The Map Shop
St. Mary's Street
P.O. Box 469
St. John's, Antigua
Tel: 462-3993

GLIMPSES OF OUR PAST
A SOCIAL HISTORY OF THE CARIBBEAN IN POSTCARDS

JOHN GILMORE

Published in Jamaica 1995 by

Ian Randle Publishers
206 Old Hope Road, Box 686
Kingston 6
© 1995 John Gilmore

All rights reserved. No part of this book may
be reproduced in any form without written
permission of the publisher and author

ISBN 976-8100-40-0

A catalogue record for this book is available
from the National Library of Jamaica.

Book & Cover Design by Michael Gordon
Printed in Hong Kong by Regent Publishing Services Ltd.

CONTENTS

INTRODUCTION v

1. The History and Appeal of the Postcard 1

2. The Sugar Industry 29

3. Other Occupations 37

4. Transport 59

5. Tourism 67

6. Historic Buildings and Monuments 77

7. Cityscapes and Street Scenes 87

8. Housing 99

9. Disasters 109

10. Religion, Festivals and Entertainment 113

11. Keeping Control 125

12. Portraits 129

Index 145

FOR MARITA AND ALEX

INTRODUCTION

About fifteen years ago, idly flipping through some old postcards in a shop in an English country town, I was suddenly confronted by one with a picture of the school in Barbados where my mother taught for many years and where I myself had taught for a brief period. It had clearly been taken a long time ago: the buildings were easily recognizable, but the figures in front of them suggested a school very different from the one I knew. On the back of the card was an attractive Barbadian stamp, from the middle of the first decade of this century.

What was such a thing doing in Canterbury? Why was there no message written on the card, just the address on the back? I was a student of Caribbean history, but I was more accustomed to thinking of historical source material in terms of printed and manuscript documents rather than of visual images of our past. In fact, there had always seemed to be hundreds of pages of official reports, thousands and thousands of unadorned words, to every painting or engraving of a West Indian scene, a caricature of a ball at King's House in Jamaica, perhaps, or a windmill at work on an Antiguan plantation.

I bought the card (1a and 1b). My curiosity aroused, I started looking for others. I soon found that collecting old postcards was a fairly new but rapidly growing hobby. Almost every town in England seemed to have a stamp shop which sold postcards as a sideline; there were dealers who sold nothing else to be met at antique fairs and flea markets. And in among all the other cards -- the music-hall stars, the coronation portraits of King Edward VII or King George V, the scenes of the Japan-British exhibition of 1910, the patriotic images from the First World War, the African missions, the Chinese executions, the horse-drawn trams and steam locomotives, the streets in London, Paris, Rome -- there would almost always be one or two of somewhere in the Caribbean. And since contemporary Caribbean postcards in the late 1970s and early 1980s usually showed nothing more interesting than a stretch of beach and a few palm trees, I was astonished by the variety of the older cards. The beach scenes and the tropical sunsets were there, yes, but so too were the views of the sugar industry when windmills still ground cane in Barbados, of every imaginable form of agriculture from growing Easter lilies in Bermuda to raising ostriches in Curacao, the streets of Port of Spain or Castries or St. John's, the great Kingston earthquake of 1907, markets in Paramaribo or St. George's, milk sellers, pottery vendors and firemen, the houses of rich and poor ...

There are so many old postcards around because they were avidly collected when they were new. The postcard album was the television documentary of its day; when mass tourism meant railway trips to the nearest seaside resort and cheap air travel remained several decades in the future, the picture postcard was one of the few ways people had of knowing what distant countries looked like. Collectors all over the world found each other's addresses and exchanged postcards of their respective countries (**2, 123**); the arrival of the postman and the glimpse of an exotic stamp would have been eagerly awaited (**3, 4**). There are enough postcards with nothing more than an address written on them to suggest that such collectors' friendships were often no more than simple barter arrangements; most of the messages one does find on postcards are exceedingly banal, though this is scarcely surprising in view of the semi-public nature of this type of correspondence.

How did it all start? The postcard has its predecessors, in the form of printed decorative envelopes and various types of official printed stationery, but it is generally agreed that the first postcard was one issued by the authorities in Austria-Hungary on 1 October 1869. It was not what many people in the Caribbean call a 'view-card'; it was a piece of thin card which had on one side a stamp with a portrait of the Emperor Franz-Josef (which was printed directly onto the card) and the inscription 'Correspondenz-Karte' with a small version on the imperial coat-of-arms, and a space for the address, all inside a decorative border, while the message was to be written on the other side.

The new invention was cheap and convenient for short messages, and was extremely popular from the start, with millions sent through the post in the first year. Postal authorities in other countries soon followed the example of Austria-Hungary and issued postcards of their own; Britain did so in October 1870, while in June 1871 Canada became the first country outside Europe to issue postcards. These early cards were all intended for use only within their country of origin, and it was not until after 22 countries formed the General Postal Union (later the Universal Postal Union) in 1875 that cards came into use which could be sent to foreign countries. By the 1880s, the postcard had reached the Caribbean. Some early examples are what are known as 'formula cards' -- the card has an inscription printed on it, but the stamps are ordinary adhesive postage stamps which were stuck onto the card before it was issued by the Post Office (5). These were soon replaced by ones which had the stamp printed directly onto the card (6-8).

The earliest postcards were all government issued and, apart from the stamps and perhaps a small coat-of-arms, had no pictures at all. Privately issued postcards originated in the United States, with the first known postally used examples dating from about a year after the first Austrian official cards; they were introduced in Britain in June 1872. Advertisements began to appear (at first printed onto officially issued postcards) almost immediately, and are found in Britain from 1870. At about the same date, decorative illustrations began to appear on postcards published in continental Europe, and by the early 1890s many attractive pictorial cards were available, often with beautifully printed vignettes of topographical scenes.

In Britain, however, postal regulations for several years remained more restrictive than those on the continent. It was not until September 1894 that the British authorities allowed the issue of privately printed cards onto which the buyer could stick an ordinary halfpenny stamp bought from the Post Office. This made the production of decorative postcards worthwhile for the commercial publisher, but it still took a few years for the idea to really catch on in Britain. There was also the problem that British regulations insisted on smaller cards than those used in Europe, which of course meant less room for pictures. A new slightly larger card, called 'court size', was introduced in Britain in January 1895, but at 4½ by 3½ inches (115 by 90mm) this was still an inch shorter than the European ones. It was not until November 1899 that British postcard publishers were allowed to issue cards in the larger size 5½ by 3½ inches, or 140 by 90mm, which had been in use in European countries for several years, and which became a more or less worldwide standard until recent times.

There was one further obstacle to the full development of the picture postcard. As long as nothing more than the address and a stamp was supposed to go on one side of the card, there was a limit to how much of the other side could be used for a picture -- either some space had to be left for a message, or the sender would be forced to write over the picture. In 1902 a British publisher introduced cards which had a line printed down the back, dividing the right-hand side (still reserved for the address and the stamp) from the left-hand side where space was now available for a message. Once this was done, it was possible for the whole of the other side to be taken up by a picture. This of course is the system we know today. The new invention was accepted fairly quickly by the postal authorities in Britain; such cards were in circulation by the second half of 1902, and over the next few years came into general use in other countries.

The postcard in the Caribbean followed a similar progress, although changes seemed to have lagged slightly behind those in the metropolitan countries. Early cards from the British colonies are found in court size (8, 9), and the 'undivided back' is at first standard, so that (sometimes considerable) space for the message is left on the picture side (10, 11). The 'divided back' (12) came into use at about the same time as it became standard elsewhere, however, and any Caribbean card with an undivided back is unlikely to be much later than about 1907 (though of course some cards would have been sent through the post several years after they were produced).

Most collectors would agree that the 'Golden Age' of the postcard was the period up to 1914. The horrors of the First World War gave people other things to think about, and the widespread enthusiasm for postcard collecting dwindled considerably. There was also the practical point that, as a result of their early specialization in the field, German printers had produced a large proportion of the world's picture postcards -- innumerable cards from local publishers in the British Caribbean colonies have 'Printed in Saxony' or 'Printed in Germany' on them somewhere in tiny letters. The war put a stop to this, at least temporarily. Finally, after the war, postage rates went up in many countries, further reducing the popularity of the postcard.

In terms of both quantity and quality, the period from about 1900 to 1914 is the one most likely to command the attention of the postcard collector interested in the Caribbean. Here, as in other parts of the world, postcards continued to be produced in the 1920s, '30s and '40s, some of them of considerable merit, but the collector does not seem to come across them as often as those of the earlier period. From the 1950s, the quality of postcards shows a marked decline. This is found elsewhere, not just in the Caribbean, though here the rapid growth of tourism which came with comparatively cheap air travel seems to have encouraged a proliferation of the beach and palm trees type of card. Nevertheless, a sharp eye can still sometimes spot an interesting detail in a card from the 1960s which at first sight appears extremely dull. There has been a dramatic change for the better in recent years and, although insipid, stereotyped beach scenes are still on the market, many excellent postcards are now produced by photographers and publishers all over the region.

What sort of things can someone interested in older cards published or used in the Caribbean expect to find? I have yet to see from the Caribbean some of the novelty cards found from elsewhere (such as leather postcards or postcards which include a small 78 r.p.m. record), but most types can be found. There are panoramic cards, which fold out to two or three times the normal width (13), fantasy cards (14), and cards for special occasions such as Christmas or weddings (16). Coats-of-arms appear on postcards (17, 19), as do maps (18, 20). There are various types of advertising cards (22, 23). With some cards, the decoration may be more interesting than the pictures (21), while there may be more to other cards than at first appears (24a and 24b). There are religious cards (25, 26), art cards (30) and humorous cards -- though the humour is often of a sort distasteful to modern sensibilities (27 to 29). 'Real photo' cards were produced directly from the original negative rather than by a commercial printing process (33). **Some cards serve as indicators of environmental change (31)**, while others have the intimate appeal of the family snapshot (33, 34). A card may command attention because it is the work of a named photographer (37) or because it shows some familiar location which has changed drastically since the card was published (38). There seem to be few parts of the Caribbean of which you will not see an old postcard sooner or later (39), and a great many cards, including those dealing with subjects such as tourism, the sugar industry or other forms of agriculture, could be classed simply as topographical. Postcards which show close-ups of individuals or small groups have a special appeal (see particularly 213 to 240). If you are very lucky, you may come across a postcard written by or addressed to some locally or regionally famous figure, and many cards are of interest in one way or another to postal history collectors. Some cards of course have several different points of interest at once (42a and 42b).

A serious look at any substantial collection of old postcards soon leads to a number of questions. Most basically, does a card show what it purports to show? In a few cases, a card is simply baffling (40). Some cards have been fairly obviously retouched (143, for example); in some cases one wonders whether things which were never in the picture to start with have been put in later (41a and 41b).

Unlike an album of family snapshots, or a portfolio of one photographer's work, a collection of postcards is a selection of published images intended for widespread consumption. Who decided which cards to publish? For whom were the postcards intended? Some postcards of the Caribbean were published outside the region, catering to the market for images of exotic, faraway places. A great many of these came from the British firm of Raphael Tuck & Sons Ltd., which published enormous numbers of almost every conceivable type of postcard, including photographic scenes and artists' impressions of places all over the globe. A specialist in the Caribbean was Algernon Aspinall, who from London published many 'West Indian Picture Postcards' as well as a popular tourist guidebook to the islands.

On the other hand, a high proportion -- to judge from those I have seen, an absolute majority -- of all early postcards relating to the Caribbean are the work of local publishers (and, presumably, local photographers), albeit in many cases printed outside the region. Some Caribbean photographers and publishers moved beyond the purely local; the Antiguan photographer José Anjo, for example, produced postcards of several different islands. Postcards were used locally as a convenient means of communication in the days when few people had a telephone, and even a business house might send a customer a message on a picture postcard (8). Postcards -- sometimes with what might seem to us bizarrely inappropriate subjects -- were used to send birthday or Christmas greetings to friends or relatives in the same island (240).

Nevertheless, the demand for postcards was restricted to the better off. The usual cost of a picture postcard in the Caribbean was probably the same as it was in Britain in the early years of the 20th century: 'Penny plain, or twopence coloured' -- two cents or four cents. It might cost only a halfpenny to send a postcard locally, or a penny to send it anywhere else in the world (1¢ or 2¢), but for a labourer who was lucky to get 24¢ for a day's work the cost of a card and of mailing it would have seemed a lot of money. And while tourism has a long history in the Caribbean -- George Washington has a claim to be considered as the patron saint of the region's tourism (132, 133) -- until about the 1950s it was largely a matter of the sort of thing described in Aspinall's **Pocket Guide to the West Indies** or Alec Waugh's **The Sugar Islands** (New York, 1949). Waugh recalled that in 1926 he had bought a ticket for a first class round-the-world cruise and that 'a ticket that included twenty weeks' board and lodging, cost under nine hundred dollars'. He commented, 'For a writer with no responsibilities or overhead expenses ... large-scale travel provided in the 1920s a very economical design for living'. Perhaps it was for him, but the price of that ticket would have been equivalent to twelve or fifteen years' wages for an agricultural labourer in many West Indian islands.

Tourists like Waugh, whose views of a Caribbean island were formed over cocktails at a segregated club or dinner at Government House, were unlikely to have much of a profound understanding of the lives of working-class West Indians. There is plenty of evidence to suggest that middle and upper-class West Indians were frequently just as indifferent to the well-being of their poorer compatriots. Not surprisingly, postcards provide a reflection of this. Local as well as metropolitan publishers produced postcards of Black or East Indian people which referred to them in the captions as 'natives' -- a word never used of the local white population. Many cards suggest that the photographer viewed working-class subjects as 'types', rather than individuals.

Nevertheless, there is one aspect of this attitude for which the historian must be grateful. Two leading authorities on British and European cards -- William Dûval and Valerie

Monahan, writing in their **Collecting Postcards in Colour: 1894-1914** (Poole, 1978), note that 'it is difficult to find postcards showing views of the less salubrious areas in which the majority of people lived'. As far as my own observations go, this is true of the metropolitan countries. Where the Caribbean is concerned, on the other hand, while there is a visible class bias in the choice of postcard subjects -- the entertainments of the rich figure more prominently than those of the poor **(195-206)**, for example -- there are more than a few cards which illustrate clearly the occupations and living conditions of the mass of the population. It is possible to put together a collection of postcards showing the houses of ordinary people from around the Caribbean **(169-181)**; such cards show a fascinating variety in details of construction, but the overall impression is one of stark poverty, a grinding sameness of misery across the region. Those who produced and used the postcards appear to have been indifferent to this; presumably appalling housing was picturesque as long as it was in the Caribbean and not in the slums of Glasgow or London's East End, and pictures of ragged, malnourished children, or of back-breaking labour offered the charm of the exotic as long as their subjects were not white.

While the historic postcards of the Caribbean present a complacent, upper-class view of things -- though a few cards hint at the mechanisms of social control **(207-212)** -- this very complacency helps to ensure that they offer an extraordinary variety of images of the life and work of all classes of society. For the serious student of history, or for anyone interested in the development of the Caribbean in the 20th century, they are fascinating glimpses of our past.

GLIMPSES OF OUR PAST

x

POST CARD

The Address only here

1

THE HISTORY AND APPEAL OF THE POSTCARD

1a and 1b
Queen's College, Barbados, published by the local firm of J.R.H. Seifert & Co. 'Undivided back' card, postally used. The postmark is not clear but the stamp is a fine example of the Barbados 'Olive Blossom' commemorative issued in 1906. The printed line at the bottom left of the address side identifies a German printing firm and gives a serial number; the last two digits, in this case '05', identify the year the card was actually produced. But not all serial numbers on postcards are so easy to interpret.

THE HISTORY AND APPEAL OF THE POSTCARD

2
Belgian card showing the Antwerp Stock Exchange, sent by a collector called Victor van Praet to Mrs Sinckler at the Barbados Telephone Company in 1905. The message (in French) scribbled on the picture side says 'Please send me a card of your country in exchange for this one'.

3
English-published card from a series showing *'Postmen of the British Empire'*, in this case *'Barbadoes' (sic)*. What may be the artist's signature appears under the gate-post at the extreme left, but it is not legible. Artistic interpretations always raise the question of how accurate they are, but in this case the details all look plausible enough, especially the fact that it is the maid going out to collect the mail for what the figure of the little girl indicates is a white upper-middle-class household. I did once have my doubts about the postman's white uniform, but compare the St. Lucian card (163) which includes what appears to be a figure wearing a similar uniform.

GLIMPSES OF OUR PAST

4
Cards showing a series of stamps were popular with early collectors and are found for many countries. This fine embossed example with undivided back shows stamps of Trinidad, including definitives from the series issued in 1896 and the 2d. commemorative issued in 1898 for the 400th anniversary of the landing of Columbus. No printer or publisher's name is given, but the card was almost certainly produced in Germany.

5
So-called formula card from Barbados, about 1880. The card is officially issued by the Post Office, but has adhesive stamps affixed. Cards of this type are eagerly sought by postal history collectors, and ones which have actually been sent through the post can be stunningly expensive.

6
Postal stationery card from Barbados, later 1880s. The stamp with the portrait of Queen Victoria is printed directly onto the card.

7
A later postal stationery card from Jamaica; the stamp shows King George V. Sent through the post in 1915 to a Miss Davies at a vicarage in England, the message on the reverse is interesting. The writer (only initials given) announces that they are moving to the Rectory at Linstead, and adds: 'This place is an important Cure and a growing place on the Railway line. We shall have two Churches one holds 500. It is 14 miles from here & there are several nice white families round'.

GLIMPSES OF OUR PAST

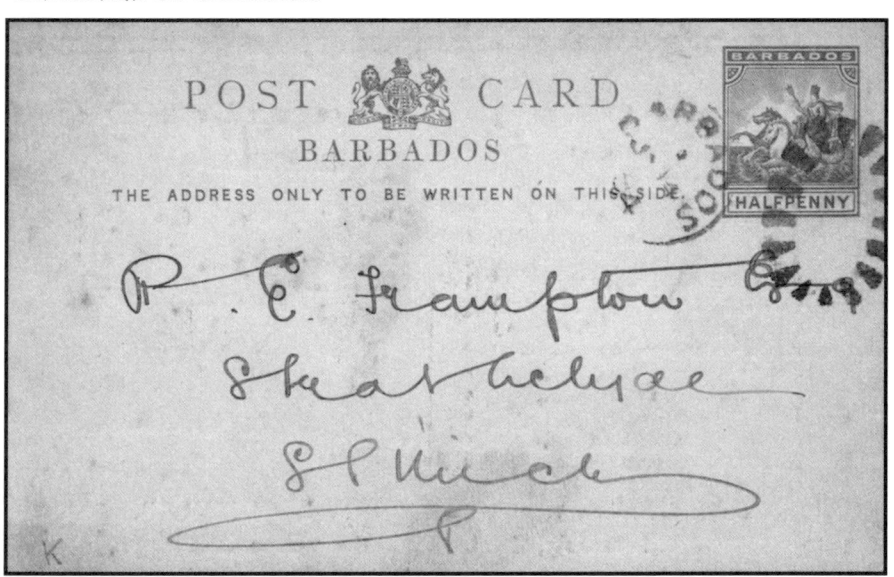

8a and 8b
Court size postal stationery card from Barbados, postally used in 1894. The reverse is a printed notice from the telephone company -- the fact that none of the phone numbers has more than three digits helps to explain why the postcard was such a popular means of communication for a long time, even for local use!

THE HISTORY AND APPEAL OF THE POSTCARD

9
Court size card with three small views of Barbados 'Broad Street', 'Bridgetown' and 'Marine Hotel' and space for little more than 'Just a word' by way of a message. Sent through the post in 1901, at which date regulations still forbade anything except the address on the other side of the card.

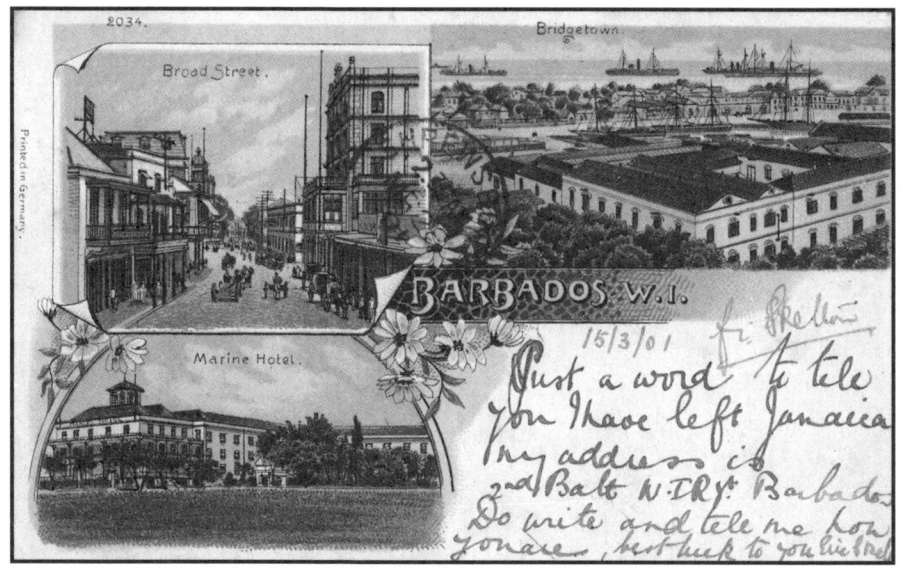

10
'Undivided back' card from Barbados, probably not later than 1905. Two small views of 'The Crane Coast' and 'Lord's Castle, Barbados' are arranged to leave plenty of space for a message.

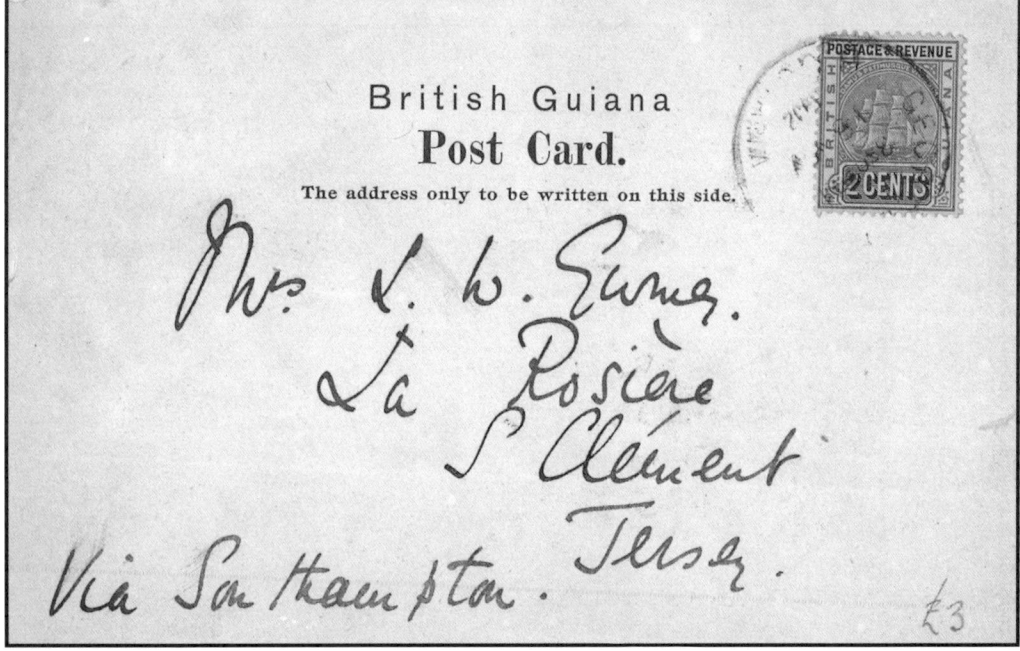

11a and 11b
Early 'undivided back' card from British Guiana, showing the Town Hall in Georgetown and posted to a corespondent in Jersey, Channel Islands in 1902. Along the left-hand edge of the picture side is a printed line with a serial number, the statement 'printed in Germany' and the name of a local publisher, in this case H.K.L. v. Ziegesar, Georgetown. This combination of foreign printing with local publication is extremely common, even up to today.

12a and 12b
An early 'divided back' card from Grenada. Note the printed line dividing the back of the card, with 'This space may be used for communication' on one side and 'The address only to be written here' on the other -- instructions repeated in one form or another on innumerable postcards to the present day. With the back divided like this, the picture (in this case, the harbour at St. George's) can fill the entire front of the card.

GLIMPSES OF OUR PAST

14
This floral bicycle ornamented with bits of glitter has a definitely Victorian feel to it, but the back of the card is divided, so it can't be too early -- perhaps somewhere between 1905 and 1910. The back also has 'Made in England' printed on it, but it is possible that the 'Fond Love From Barbados' was added to the card locally. It certainly appears to have been done by hand, whereas the bicycle itself is printed.

THE HISTORY AND APPEAL OF THE POSTCARD

13
Fold-out card, three times normal width, showing a panoramic view of St. John's, Antigua, by local photographer José Anjo. About 1905-1910.

15
'Undivided back' card showing an interpretation of the colonial badge of Barbados, with the British sovereign as Neptune, riding in a chariot formed out of a seashell and drawn by seahorses. The figure is clearly intended as a representation of Queen Victoria, and the card is unlikely to have been published very long after her death in January 1901.

GLIMPSES OF OUR PAST

16
Italian-made wedding postcard, sent with best wishes to a bride in the Dominican Republic in July 1929.

17
Another, rather later card of the Barbados badge (strictly speaking, the caption is in error in describing it as a 'coat of arms'). This reproduces the great seal of the island showing King Charles II as Lord of Barbados.

18
Reproduced at postcard size, most of the information on this map of Barbados is illegible even with a magnifying glass. Presumably you were expected to buy it because you thought it looked pretty.

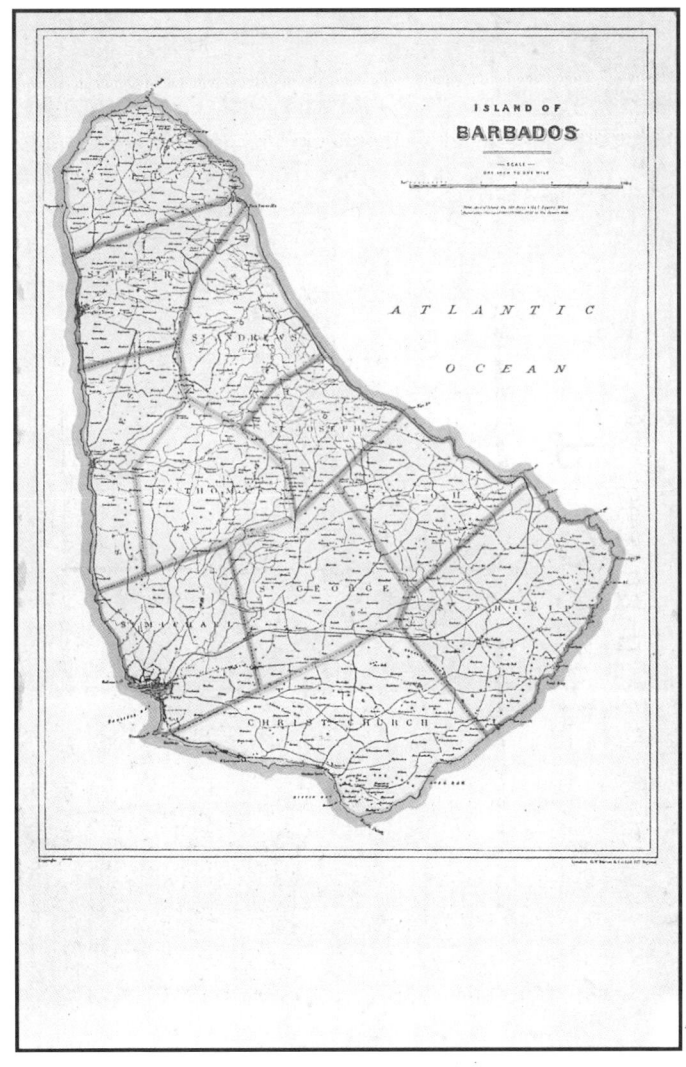

19
Coat of arms of the ill-fated Federation of the West Indies (1958-1962), published by the Federal Information Service.

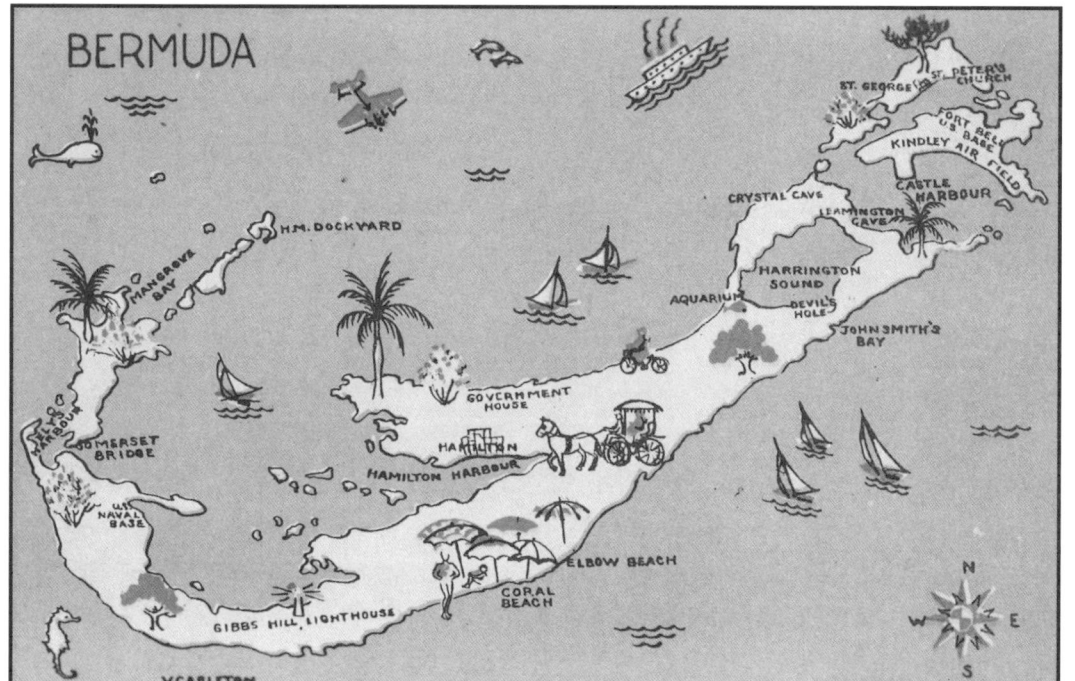

20
This much later example from Bermuda is unashamedly map as ornament. The inclusion of the US bases as well as HM Dockyard suggests a date after the Second World War, but the card still has a definite period look to it.

21
Seven small views of Barbados, on a card with some attractive *art nouveau* decoration. No indication of printer or publisher, but probably issued sometime before the First World War.

THE HISTORY AND APPEAL OF THE POSTCARD

GOVERNMENT HOUSE, PORT OF SPAIN, TRINIDAD.

22a and 22b
A fine advertisement for Trinidad cheroots, printed for the Colonial & Indian Exhibition held in England in 1905. It was probably given away on the spot, since there is no space left on the card for any other message, an address or a stamp. Traces of old gum suggest the card was once stuck into an album by an earlier collector more interested in the other side of the card -- a rather unexciting view of Government House in Port of Spain.

TRINIDAD CHEROOTS.

MADE BY
TRINIDAD LABOUR,
OF
TRINIDAD TOBACCO,
BOXED IN
TRINIDAD CEDAR.

EXHIBITED BY
WEST INDIAN TOBACCO CO. LTD.,
PORT OF SPAIN,
TRINIDAD.

COLONIAL & INDIAN EXHIBITION,
1905.

23a and 23b
A much later advertising card, with an aerial view of yet another Government House, this time the one in St. Lucia. The reverse has a *'Visit Sunny St. Lucia'* advertisement and enough blank space left for the card to be used postally. Possibly 1940s or earlier.

THE HISTORY AND APPEAL OF THE POSTCARD

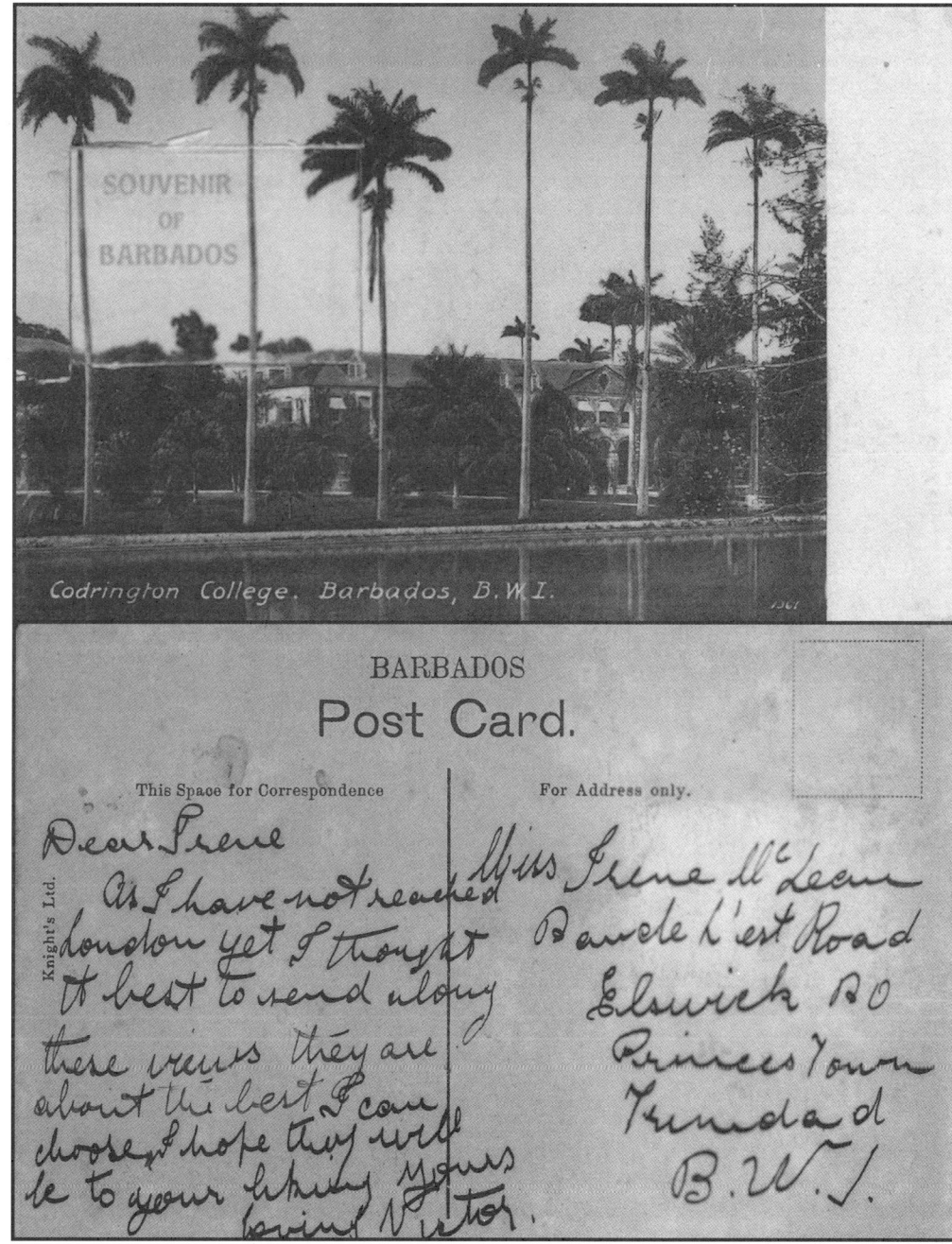

24a and 24b
Beautiful card of Codrington College, Barbados -- a popular subject found on many different cards, then and now. The panel marked 'SOUVENIR OF BARBADOS' lifts up to reveal a fold-out strip of paper with ten different views of the island, all of which were also published as full-size postcards.

25

An unusual religious card from the Caribbean, showing the Peruvian Dominican friar, the Blessed Martin de Porres (1579-1639). Printed in the United States, published by the English and Spanish Correspondence Club, Santurce, Puerto Rico.

Blessed Martin de Porres, O.P.
Apostle of Charity,
Help me.

26

View of '*A native home in Trinidad, West Indies*', this card could find a home in the religious category: it was published by the Church of England missionary organization, the Society for the Propagation of the Gospel, whose initials S.P.G. were sufficiently well known to appear on the card without further explanation.

TRINIDAD (*i.e.* Trinity Island), discovered by Columbus on Trinity Sunday, 1498. The S.P.G. supports work here and throughout the greater part of the West Indies. A branch of the King's Messengers S.P.G. has been started.

A NATIVE HOME IN TRINIDAD, WEST INDIES.

THE HISTORY AND APPEAL OF THE POSTCARD

27
This picture of two boys fighting while others watch is described as 'Copyright 1895 by F. L. Howe'. The scene is obviously posed, the background looks suspicious, and a close look makes one wonder if at least some of the figures were not in fact white boys who have been 'coloured' along with the photograph. The caption *'Who's a Nigger?'* and the information on the reverse that the card was one of a series called 'Dixie Land' from the British firm of Raphael Tuck & Sons indicate that this was one of the many cards published in the early years of this century which were designed to appeal to the racist sentiments of their purchasers. But the card's later history really attracts the attention of a Caribbean collector: in 1906 somebody posted it in Memphis, Tennessee, to a boy in Barbados ('Master Jack Barnett'); there is no message, only the name and address, and a later redirection to St. Bartholomew's Vicarage! Did the postman who had to deliver it take a good look at this curious item, and if so, what did he think?

28
The man posed with the caiman skin is captioned *'Its [sic] alright when you know him but you got to know him first!!'* with 'Jamaica' in brackets afterwards, but there is no indication of where the card was printed or published.

19

GLIMPSES OF OUR PAST

"Hog run fe life, Dawg run fe him character."

29
Posted from Jamaica to England in 1906, this cartoon with the caption *'Hog run fe life, Dawg run fe him character'* bears no indication of where it was printed or published. The artist's signature is not very legible but appears to be F. Francil or Francie. The human figures may simply be badly drawn, but it is quite possible that they were intended as racist caricatures.

30
Reproductions of works of art are common on postcards, but it is not often that you find one from a Caribbean source. This painting of the Resurrection by the American-born British artist Benjamin West (1738-1820) was commissioned by a Barbadian planter in 1776 and hangs in St. George's Church, Barbados. The card dates from about 1910 and on the back are printed several lines of information about the painting, taken from 'Legends of Barbados', by the local antiquarian E. G. Sinckler.

THE HISTORY AND APPEAL OF THE POSTCARD

31
This view of the Holetown River catches the attention of any Barbadian familiar with the miserably tiny patch of polluted swamp on the coast which is all that remains here. Postcards recording similar environmental changes can probably be found for many Caribbean countries.

32
Official documents, such as the commissions of colonial governors, used to refer to 'Barbados and its dependencies.' The largest of these was Pelican Island, a small island just off the shore at Fontabelle on the outskirts of Bridgetown. Some visitors became more familiar with it than they might have wished, because for many years it served as a quarantine station. It was perhaps last used for this purpose during an outbreak of meningitis in Barbados in the 1940s.

Pelican Island no longer has a separate existence, as it was joined to the mainland during the construction of the Deep Water Harbour (1956-61)

Note the curious copyright line, which identifies the local photographer, Alfred Bayley, and gives the month and day, but not the year (though the card dates from about 1910).

33
A 'real photo' card, this charming mother and child study looks like a family snapshot, but it is produced in postcard format, and indeed has 'POST CARD' printed on the back, where someone has added the handwritten inscription 'With love Winnie, "Bubbles" '6 months'. Difficult to date, but 1940s or 1950s would be a good guess.

34
Real photo card from the 1920s or 1930s, showing a middle-class residence identified as Lyonville, Barbados. Note the Union Jack on the flagstaff. The card was almost certainly privately produced in very small quantities for use by the family which lived in the house.

THE HISTORY AND APPEAL OF THE POSTCARD

35
Port au Prince, Haiti, from the sea. A good example of an 'Oilette' card from the British firm of Raphael Tuck & Sons, who published enormous numbers of artists' impressions of scenes in many different parts of the world in the early years of this century.

36
A 'tropical landscape' at Punta Inglesa, Dominican Republic (about 1940). I first thought this was an artist's impression, but closer examination suggests that it started out as a genuine photograph, to which some rather lurid artificial colouring was later added.

GLIMPSES OF OUR PAST

Crane Hotel, Barbados, B.W.I.

37
Crane Hotel, Barbados. A fine study by the well-known local photographer H. W. Parkinson, who is acknowledged on the reverse.

38
Constitution River, Barbados (card posted in 1913). Most Barbadians of the present era are astonished by the thought that this was once wide enough to have boats on it. Later canalization has reduced the river to little more than a broad drain.

Constitution River, Barbados.

39
Early 'undivided back' card showing oyster beds in *'Carriacon' (sic)*. There is probably no part of the Caribbean of which you will not see an old postcard sooner or later.

40
With its seemingly unrelated fragments of three or possibly four different pictures ('Washer Women, Barbados', a bandstand which is perhaps that at Hastings on the island's south coast, the bottom part of a street scene with a row of bicycles parked against a building and an ornamental pattern in one corner), this card appears to be a mistake which should never have left the printer. Yet somebody called Myrtle sent it through the post to a friend as a Christmas card.

August-holiday Merry Making. A native dance

41a and 41b
Jamaican card, printed in Berlin and published by the Educational Supply Co. The caption reads: *'August holiday Merry Making. A native dance'*. You do not have to look very hard to realize that the original picture has been heavily retouched. The two seated figures playing accordions (towards the right-hand edge) look suspiciously Germanic and might have escaped from a fête in the Black Forest. Were they in the original scene at all?

THE HISTORY AND APPEAL OF THE POSTCARD

42a and 42b
Exceptional card captioned *'Donkey Cart Stand, Barbados'*. A little local knowledge allows us to identify the scene as Trafalgar Square in Bridgetown (now Parliament Square), but it has changed almost beyond recognition. The donkey carts have long gone, like the horse-drawn cabs in the background and the building behind them; only the older generation can remember the tree, the crane at the left, or the days when schooners could still be seen in the Careenage. The tourist's comment on the picture side is not without interest: 'This island is a beautifully small one and is one of the healthiest places in the Americas. A negro population predominates'. But for the serious postal history collector, the best part is on the reverse, where a pair of Barbados halfpenny stamps have a New York Post Office Hudson Terminal Station Paquebot cancellation, indicating that the card was actually posted on board ship on its way to an address in Canada.

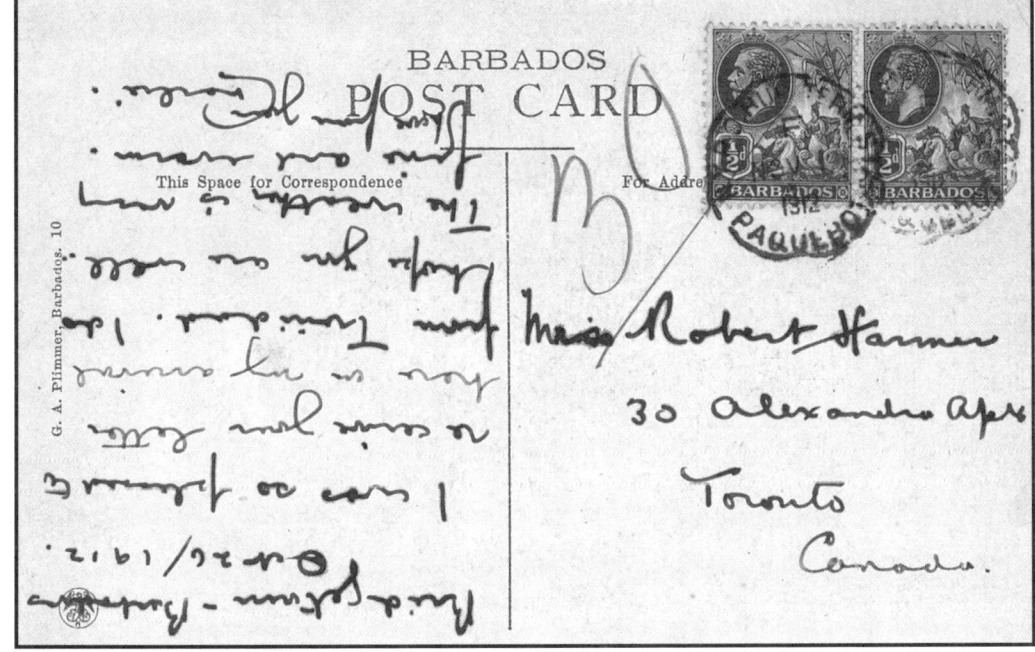

GLIMPSES OF OUR PAST

43
Card showing River Road, Barbados, postally used in 1906 and possibly printed a couple of years earlier. There is plenty of other evidence to confirm the impressive width of the Constitution river in days gone by (compare 38), but the 'mountain' in the top left never existed, and seems to be the result of the picture being over-enthusiastically touched up. Perhaps it was somebody at the German printers who thought that all tropical landscapes ought to have mountains!

POST CARD

The Address only here

2

THE SUGAR INDUSTRY

44
Early 'undivided back' from Jamaica, sent to England in 1902. Note the 'Greetings from Jamaica' slogan. The group has obviously been asked to pose for the camera, but the scene looks authentic, and the expressions appear to be genuine: the smile on the face of the man in the middle and the way he holds his machete suggests that it might have been a welcome break from actually cutting cane; the woman to his left looks a little apprehensive; and there is a striking dignity in the face of the older woman bending at the right of the picture.

45
Another 'undivided back' from the same Jamaican publisher A. Duperly & Sons; postally used (to Greece) in 1905, though the original photograph may have been taken a little earlier. Rather more artificial than the previous group: several are holding pieces of cane to their mouths in less than convincing poses; sucking cane seems to have been the sort of 'native custom' photographers thought would appeal to potential buyers of their pictures (compare 237). Look at the white or light-skinned man in hat, jacket and bow-tie; overseer, manager or estate owner? He has a noticeable case of what older Barbadians used to refer to as 'manager belly'!

THE SUGAR INDUSTRY

46a and 46b
A later and much more natural Jamaican view of the crop season, identified by the caption as Hartlands, St. Catherine. Postally used to England in 1929, the post-mark provides an ironic contrast to the picture side, as it invites the recipient to *'Spend your vacation in summerland Jamaica'*.

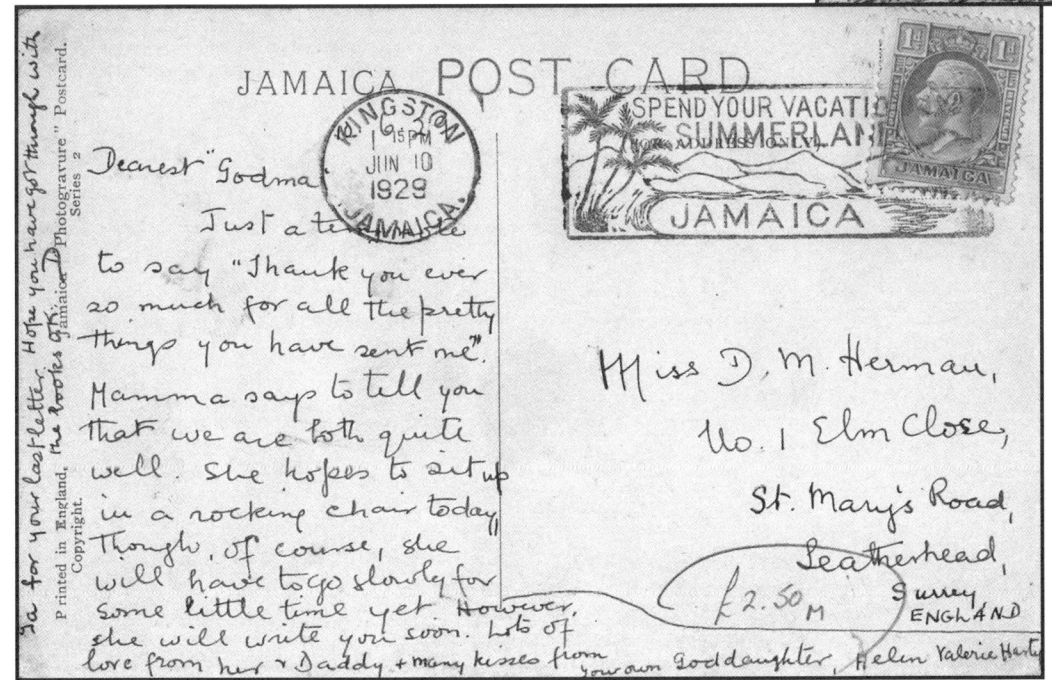

"Woodlands" Sugar Estate, Grenada

47
Beautiful tinted view of Woodlands Sugar Estate, Grenada. The sugar factory looks comparatively modern, but the card itself is an 'undivided back' probably produced before 1905. Unusual to find a sugar factory shown like this in its landscape setting.

48
Card of Cattle Mill used for crushing Sugar Cane, St. Lucia. This example was postally used in 1913, but the mill itself is of a type used in the Caribbean since the early 16th century. The cattle move round in a circle, attached to the long poles, and so turn a set of (usually) three vertical wooden rollers, through which the cane was fed by hand. Note the ox-drawn cart at the bottom right.

Cattle Mill used for crushing Sugar Cane, St. Lucia

THE SUGAR INDUSTRY

49
Similar mill, this time turned by mules, from Grenada. A rather later card, but much more of a close-up -- you can actually make out the canes between the rollers.

PRIMITIVE SUGAR MILL, GRENADA, W.I.

50
Lovely picture of a sugar windmill in Barbados, by W. G. Cooper. Even by about 1910, when this card was made, it could safely be described as the 'old process', but there were still many working windmills in the island. The reason there are so many people standing around is that the mill is not actually working -- it is much more likely that the photographer waited for a lull in the wind than that the mill was stopped for his benefit. There are plenty of canes waiting to be ground.

GLIMPSES OF OUR PAST

51
Another view of a modern sugar factory, sent through the post as a New Year's card for 1918. The fact that the location -- Kendal in Barbados -- is identified is a definite plus.

52
Fine view of the Basseterre sugar factory, St. Kitts. Postally used from St. Kitts to Belgium in 1914, the message on the reverse says 'I do hope you will like the three views sent', which, combined with the signature 'W. P. Pearce, Postmaster' suggests that it was despatched in response to a request from a collector. The postmaster may even have been personally responsible for the neat placing of the stamp on the picture side and the clarity of the post-mark -- all factors to increase the card's value to a collector. Completed in 1912, this factory is still in operation.

THE SUGAR INDUSTRY

53
Hauling molasses by spider, Barbados. Invented in the island, the spider was a device for making it easier to move a puncheon of molasses or rum using only the power of human muscles. The donkey-cart, the early motor-car, and the *Veedol* advertisement painted on the wall at the top right are all nice extras in this card.

HAULING MOLASSES BY SPIDER, BARBADOS.

Wind Mill Sugar Estate, Barbados, B.W.I.

54
This postcard of a Wind Mill Sugar Estate in Barbados (perhaps 1930s) makes a good symbol of economic change. Although the card does not tell you so, this is in fact Heywoods, where the factory buildings are gone, but the mill-wall still stands, stripped of its sails and machinery -- preserved as a piece of decoration in the middle of a modern tourist resort. Note the heaps of bagasse and the motor-car.

55a and 55b
The sugar industry needed enormous numbers of barrels, for both rum and molasses; these were normally assembled on the plantations from imported hoops and staves. The cooper was a skilled and comparatively well paid man, but this Barbadian card consigns him to a symbolic anonymity -- you have to look hard to spot him in front of the pile of barrels, towards the right hand edge.

POST CARD

The Address only here

3

OTHER OCCUPATIONS

Harvest of the Golden Bean, Grenada

56
Harvest of the Golden Bean, Grenada. In the early years of this century cocoa was much more important to the economies of Grenada and Trinidad than it is today. There are eleven figures visible in this card; at least two, and possibly three, appear to be doing nothing other than standing around giving instructions to the others.

57
Cowa Drying, Grenada. Mis-spellings in captions, such as this one, where 'cowa' is given for 'cocoa', are not uncommon in early West Indian cards, and are apparently the result of so many of them being printed in Germany. The name 'Stern & Schiele, Schoneberg-Berlin' on the reverse is almost certainly that of the printer of this card; it was most likely sold by a firm in Grenada, although a local publisher is not named. The cocoa beans were spread out to dry in the sun on the large rectangular trays clearly visible in the picture. These were designed so that they could easily be pushed in under the adjoining roofed structure in the event of rain. Similar arrangements can still be found today.

Cowa Drying, Grenada

OTHER OCCUPATIONS

58
'Trinidad Cocoa — Opening the pods and Extracting the Beans.' One of a set of six cards of the Trinidad cocoa industry, published together with an explanatory leaflet by the Imperial Institute in London (perhaps in the 1920s). The leaflet notes that 'The pods are collected in heaps and opened for the extraction of the "beans" which, when fresh, are covered with a pulp. The extracted "beans" are thrown into a heap or bin to ferment, or "sweat" for from 4 to 5 days'.

59
A beautiful card of workers shelling nutmegs in Grenada, perhaps about 1910. Everyone is more or less looking at the camera, though the blur of movement on some of the figures suggests that the photographer was a bit of an interruption.

60
Ploughing in St. Croix. It looks like three men and eight oxen were needed to manoeuvre a small plough which probably took a day to do what a modern tractor could do in half an hour. A nice Danish West Indian stamp on the reverse, and postally used to Barbados in 1910.

61
This odd card from Barbados was postally used to England in 1909. The caption says *Goat milking, Barbados* but the man appears to be clutching the goat by the hind leg, and there is no sign of a pail or anything else for the goat to be milked into. No one has ever been able to give me a suggestion as to the probable purpose of the conical structure which takes up most of the picture.

OTHER OCCUPATIONS

62
An unusual scene, and an unusually informative caption. Not only does it say *'Shipping Cotton & Lime Juice, Plymouth, Montserrat, B.W.I.'* but it also tells us the ship and the date: *'Per S/S Ingoma -- 19.10.35'*. Before tourism and off-shore banking, cotton and lime juice were mainstays of the Montserrat economy. Most of what is visible in this picture appears to be cotton, neatly packaged in bales. Note the rails along the jetty, for transporting goods on small hand-carts; there are cranes at the end for lowering them into the small boats (some of which can be seen) which would be used to take everything out to the waiting cargo ship, berthed some distance off in deeper water. There are two small sailing vessels to be seen, but neither of these will be the *Ingoma*, which may be somewhere out of the picture, or has perhaps not arrived yet.

63
Cotton pickers, Barbados. A major crop in Barbados in the late 18th century, cotton was also of some significance in the island in the early 1900s. However, attempts to revive the industry in more recent years have had limited success.

GLIMPSES OF OUR PAST

64
Ostriches on a farm in Curaçao, probably photographed in the 1920s, when ostrich feathers were much in demand for trimming ladies' fashions in North America and Europe. Perhaps they are making a comeback -- a new ostrich farm has been started in Curaçao recently.

65
Coconut estate in Trinidad, from a card printed and apparently published in England; postally used there in 1925.

OTHER OCCUPATIONS

66
Artist's impression of *Gathering cocoanuts (sic)* in St. Lucia. A Tuck's 'Oilette' card, published in England.

67
Banana Carriers, Kingston, Jamaica, by H. S. Duperly.

68
Early 'undivided back' of rope tobacco sellers in Jamaica, by A. Duperly & Sons.

69
Attractive card of Picking Pimento in Jamaica. Dr Jas. Johnson, Brown's Town P.O., whose name is printed on the back, was perhaps both photographer and publisher.

OTHER OCCUPATIONS

70
Packing tea in Jamaica. A Tuck card published in England; the reverse prints the name *Blossom Brand Jamaica Tea* and gives the addresses Claremont, Jamaica and 154, Church Road, Hove, Sussex.

Packing Jamaica Blossom Brand Tea.

Easter Lily Field, Belle Vue, Bermuda.

71
Easter Lily Field, Belle Vue, Bermuda.

45

72
View of the flying fish fleet in Barbados. The card dates from the 1930s or 1940s. In Barbados, sail-powered fishing vessels were still common in the early 1950s, but were soon afterwards replaced by motor boats.

73
Landing Flying Fish Catch, Barbados. Card perhaps from the 1920s.

OTHER OCCUPATIONS

74
Fishermen at Ste-Marie, Martinique, launching a boat. Published by Phos, Guadeloupe.

75
Card from the same publisher, with nice shot of a group of men, women and children in Guadeloupe fishing from shore with a seine-net.

47

76
Sponge clipping in the Bahamas. Natural sponges were collected and exported from the Bahamas from the 1840s, and at the beginning of the 20th century this was the island's major industry, employing about a third of the labour force. By the 1920s, however, exports were on the decline, mainly as a result of the development of natural substitutes for artificial sponges, and in 1938 the Bahamian sponges were wiped out by a fungus disease.

77
Preparing sea-eggs for market, Barbados. Over-fishing and coastal pollution mean that sea-eggs are now much less common than they once were. The face of the woman on the right looks heavily retouched.

78
Gold-washing in Suriname, from a card postally used in 1903. The long tom is the rectangular sieve through which the alluvial deposits are passed in the search for particles of gold.

79
A similar scene, with slightly more elaborate equipment, showing sluicing for diamonds on the Mazaruni River in Guyana. Postally used from Georgetown to Holland in 1906, the sender has written on the front 'Find a British Guiana diamond in this card' but it is no longer where he had taped it to the picture!

80
The Manjak mines in the Barbadian parish of St. Joseph. Manjak is a bituminous substance which was once used in road-making.

81
A stone quarry in Barbados. All the work appears to being done by men with crow-bars. Judging by the shapes left cut in the quarry walls, the aim would have been to produce blocks rather than small, loose stones. Once dug out, the rough blocks would have been cut to shape with large hand-saws, something made easier by the softness of the island's coral stone. A coral block is now normally 12" x 8" x 8" but they used to come in much larger sizes, such as 24" x 12" x 12". Note that not only does this picture suggest that all the cutting was done by hand, but also that there is no sign of even the simplest mechanical equipment for lifting the blocks, and no sign of any safety precautions either. Unusually for a card from one of the former British West Indian islands, this one is manufactured by a French firm.

82
Road making in Jamaica -- a Group of Labourers from a card apparently manufactured and sold in England. There seem to be no more than two, or possibly three, adult males in the group; all the rest are women and boys.

83
Digging pitch, Trinidad. The card may date from during or just after the First World War -- the usual discreet 'Printed in Saxony' is replaced by 'British Manufacture Throughout' although the name of a Trinidadian publisher is also given.

84
The Trinidadian oil industry: real photo card (possibly 1930s) showing a derrick in a forest clearing.

85
Another real photo card of similar date, showing the oil refinery in Curaçao. One of the largest in the world, this provided jobs for many migrant workers from the islands of the eastern Caribbean.

OTHER OCCUPATIONS

86
Before oil took over as the dominant fuel, St. Lucia was an important coaling station for steamships travelling through the Caribbean. Refuelling was done, as we see here, by women carrying the coal up into the ship in baskets on their heads; those coming down, relieved for a moment of their heavy burden, carry their empty baskets in one hand. Note the group with the parasol watching the scene in the bottom right. There are a number of cards showing similar scenes; this one is perhaps unusual in naming the ship, the U.S.S. St. Louis.

87
Group of firemen with their hand-drawn cart -- among the equipment you can make out several buckets, a quantity of what is either rope or hose, and an axe. The card gives no indication of photographer, printer or publisher, but it is probably Barbadian, and was given as a Christmas card to a Barbadian addressee one year early this century. In spite of three small worm-holes and a creased corner, the unusual subject makes this card well worth having.

53

88
Washer women, Barbados. The clothes the women are wearing certainly catch the eye, but it is also worth noting the size of the pond they are using as their water supply. Scenes like this disappeared in Barbados as virtually every rural community came to have access to piped water (even if it was only a public stand-pipe). As they ceased to have any immediate practical value, most of the island's ponds (many of which had been kept in being by careful maintenance) were allowed to dry up. Few are left in Barbados now -- unfortunately for some of the country's wildlife.

89
Washing scenes would appear to have been a popular subject. Captioned *The Tropical Laundry*, this one comes from a Grenadian publisher.

OTHER OCCUPATIONS

90
The home of Barbadian pottery is among the clay soils of the island's Scotland district. This fine card (late 1930s or 1940s) shows a man throwing a plant-pot; the seated man appears to be pulling a rope to turn the potter's wheel. The crowd is no doubt drawn by the photographer rather than by this everyday activity! A finished pot at the bottom left awaits the kiln; it has a scalloped lip of a characteristic pattern.

91
These two pottery vendors (mother and daughter? sisters?) appear on a Barbadian card postally used to New York in 1909. Each of the vendors holds a monkey, a large, unglazed, round-bellied jar once popular for storing drinking water in the days before refrigerators were in common use; some of the water would evaporate slowly through the porous clay, thus cooling what remained. More monkeys, and other examples of traditional forms of Barbadian pottery, can be seen on their wooden tray.

92
East Indian milk seller from Trinidad -- posed in the photographer's studio.

93
A Barbadian coconut vendor from a card of about the 1920's or earlier. A good example of the photographer being more interested in capturing a 'type' than an individual. No attention has been paid to the fact that the woman's face is so heavily in shadow that the features are barely discernible.

OTHER OCCUPATIONS

94
Sellers in a public market in Barbados, on a card postally used in 1924. This time the faces have come out clearly and there is good detail on the trays and their rough and ready stands -- but I can't help feeling that the photographer was unwilling to resist the temptation to retouch the costumes a bit. Look closely at the woman nearest the camera: the folds in the dress look too good to be true, and there is something a bit odd about the way her hand comes out of the sleeve.

95
A somewhat earlier Barbadian card (about 1905-1910) with a group of street sellers. Again, there may be more to this than is apparent at first sight. They have clearly been asked to pose (note how the one on the left stands with her foot up on a stool or something of the sort); how did the photographer get them together? Did they all live in the same house or sell at the same spot? The face of the woman on the right looks retouched; perhaps the tray on her head cast too much shadow. Individually, at least, the figures look convincing. The woman seated in the middle seems to be selling ribbons and other fabric trimmings, but it is hard to make out what the others are offering.

GLIMPSES OF OUR PAST

MAUBY VENDOR, BARBADOS.

96
Street vendors of many kinds were, and are a familiar feature of Caribbean life, and are found on many cards. This mauby vendor appears on a Barbadian card sent home to the USA by a visitor in 1939; a classic tourist comment 'This is an English possession honey and this is a typical street scene' forms part of the message scrawled on the back. An astringent decoction prepared from the bark of a tree, mauby is still popular in Barbados, but the traditional mauby vendor, with her heavy can balanced on top of her head is no more.

POST CARD

The Address only here

4

TRANSPORT

97
Two Suriname Maroons in their dugout canoe, on the way to Paramaribo; This card was used to Holland in 1907, and perhaps posted at sea -- but as is often the case, somebody removed the stamp a long time ago and the postmarks are not as clear as one would like.

98
A somewhat larger dugout, this time with a sail, on the Demerara River in Guyana.

TRANSPORT

99
A fine collection of sailing vessels by the Custom House in Port of Spain, Trinidad. 'undivided back', probably not much later than about 1905.

100
Another Trinidadian card of the same period, showing steam vessels at the St. Vincent Jetty.

GLIMPSES OF OUR PAST

101
A Speightstown schooner entering the Careenage at Bridgetown, Barbados. Specially built for the coastal trade, these schooners could cover the fourteen miles or so between the island's two main towns in forty minutes with a good wind. Everything goes by road now, but with today's traffic the motorist will often be hard put to better this time.

102
Lovely card with a large steamship in the inner harbour at St. George's Grenada. Undivided back.

103
A much later card with an artist's impression of one of the 'Lady boats' of the Canadian National Steamships which provided regular services between the British Caribbean islands and North America in the 1940s and 1950s.

104
Going to Town -- by ox-cart, Cuba. An 'undivided back' produced for a company in New York, but apparently manufactured in Germany.

Cocoa Boucan, Grenada

105
The woman riding a donkey in this 'undivided back' card from Grenada looks as though she might have been caught by the photographer rather than posed. The caption *Cocoa Boucan, Grenada* suggests he was more interested in the estate buildings behind.

106
Even in days gone by, one seldom saw a Bajan actually riding a donkey -- the donkey cart was much preferred as a means of transportation. Although one is reluctant to admit it, this was so because much of Barbados is rather flat in comparison with many other Caribbean islands. Note the original caption *Native Carter, Barbados* on this card, which was probably published in the 1920s or 1930s. Once common, the donkey cart is now a rare sight in Barbados.

NATIVE CARTER, BARBADOS.

107
View of the corner of Pine Road in Belleville, Barbados, with horse-drawn tram. The driver is in shadow, but can be picked out by his white pith helmet. The conductor standing on the running board is also wearing one. Postally used from Barbados to Cayenne at the end of 1910, this card was also published in a coloured version.

108
Exceptional view showing a train of the Barbados Railway, crossing a bridge near Belleplaine. It was sent through the post as a Christmas card in 1916, but the original photograph may be several years earlier.

GLIMPSES OF OUR PAST

109
This ambulance 'From the people of Barbados' was probably a gift made during the First World War. Almost certainly photographed in Britain, where the card was printed.

110
Interesting collection of motor-cars outside the Aquatic Club in Barbados, perhaps 1930s. Some of the numbers on the licence plates are clearly discernable, and an assiduous local historian might be able to identify the original owners!

POST CARD

The Address only here

5

TOURISM

111
'Undivided back' of the Annandale waterfall in Grenada, complete with (in the bottom right-hand corner) three rather overdressed gentlemen visiting it.

112
Stone with Carib Hieroglyphics, Rutland Vale. This card was printed in Germany for a firm in St. Vincent, but postally used in Barbados in 1910. The original photograph is probably a few years earlier, as the card was an undivided back. The sender drew a line down the middle by hand and used the left side for the message in the way that had become usual by the date the card was used. The men look as though they made a special trip to see the stone and are quite pleased with themselves as a result.

TOURISM

114
Princess Hotel, Bermuda. Coloured card with undivided back, postally used to the USA in 1910.

113
A real photo card (probably 1930s) showing *Sunset in the Gulf of Paria, Trinidad, B.W.I.* We must all have seen innumerable modern variations on this theme.

GLIMPSES OF OUR PAST

115
The Colonial Hotel in Nassau, The Bahamas. An attractive sepia card published in England by Tuck's.

116
Card probably from the later 1930s or 1940s with views of the Hotel Royal, Barbados. The shot of the hotel bedroom is fairly unusual. Not postally used, but the reverse has a rubber stamp from the Information Bureau at the baggage warehouse in Bridgetown, suggesting that the card was used as a publicity handout.

117
Lovely card of the Hotel Nacional in Havana. The caption printed on the reverse proudly claims *El Hotel Nacional de Cuba es el mas excelente de toda la América Latina.* Note the aircraft in the background, and El Morro can be made out on the horizon at right.

118
Once one of the great hotels in the early days of Jamaica's tourist industry, the Hotel Titchfield is long gone.

GLIMPSES OF OUR PAST

119
Also vanished is the Myrtle Bank Hotel in Kingston, probably THE hotel in Jamaica in its day. One of the 'Greetings from Jamaica' series published by A. Duperly & Son, Kingston.

120
The Myrtle Bank swimming pool.

TOURISM

121
The 'Greetings from Jamaica' series also included a number of picturesque views of the island's scenic attractions, such as this one of the Blue Hole at Port Antonio.

122
Nice view of the town of Port Antonio, from the same series.

123
The Queen's Park Hotel, Port of Spain, Trinidad.
This is an attractive card postally used to a correspondent in Brighton, England, in 1907. The message gives an interesting glimpse of postcard collecting in those days: 'Thanks for cards they are O.K. When you are at home you can post me views & scenery of Brighton, and when you are at College you can post scenery etc. of the immediate vicinity, and in case they get exhausted you can send me Actresses -- stamps always view side'.

124
This superficially rather dull card repays closer study: it shows the 'Visitors' Information and Advice Bureau' of the Barbados Publicity Committee at the old Baggage Warehouse in Bridgetown, and probably dates from the late 1930s. For many visitors to the island, this would have been their first source of information. A board with messages and letters for incoming passengers can be made out at the back of the booth on the right. On the counter at the front, stacks of leaflets and a revolving rack with picture postcards are clearly visible. At the extreme right is what looks as though it might be a glass case with a stuffed flying fish.

TOURISM

125
The less desirable side of tourism: 'Diving Boys' from a 'West indian view Postcard' published in England by Raphael Tuck & Sons. Boys and young men swam or paddled small boats out to visiting ships and dived for coins thrown overboard by the passengers. A risky and to many minds demeaning way of earning a pittance, but there were few opportunities for these children.

Diving Boys. West Indies

126
A good laugh for all, or selling one's soul for the tourist dollar? The Haunted Wood on a Barbadian undivided back card of 1905. There is a small white blur in the background which is presumably meant to be the 'ghost'.

127
The Cannibal Canal in Barbados, like the Haunted Wood, was an invention of Mr. Pomeroy, the American-born proprietor of the Marine Hotel at the turn of the century and intended to amuse his guests. The 'ghosts' and 'cannibals' were members of Mr. Pomeroy's staff.

POST CARD

The Address only here

6

HISTORIC BUILDINGS AND MONUMENTS

128
One of the most recent cards in this book, but one of the oldest European structures in the Caribbean: the back of the card calls it *'Castillo de Cristobal Colon'*, but it is in fact the Alcazar in Santo Domingo, Dominican Republic, built by Christopher Columbus's son Diego in 1510, shown sometime before the building was restored in 1955. The card also gives the capital the name Ciudad Trujillo which it bore during the rule of the dictator Rafael Leonidas Trujillo (1930-1961); the car in the bottom right suggests a date in the 1940s or 1950s.

129
Fine real photo card of El Morro, Havana.

HISTORIC BUILDINGS AND MONUMENTS

130
Not a lot of detail visible in this Guyanese card showing the seventeenth-century *Ruins of an Old Dutch Fort on Fort Island, River Essequibo, once the Seat of the Government of the Colony.*

131
The tree does a good job of obscuring this view of Holborn House, which was built in 1648 and used as the residence of the governor of Barbados for some thirty years in the seventeenth century. Nevertheless, an interesting card of an important building which has since been demolished.

132
'Undivided back' card, perhaps about 1905, showing 'Geo Washington's home when in Barbados'. Note the coachman and buggy under the trees at the left. This may possibly be Bush Hill House at the Garrison, which still stands in somewhat altered form, and which modern research (by Michael Chandler and Peter Campbell) has conclusively proved to have been the actual house occupied by George Washington and his brother Lawrence during their visit to Barbados in 1751. Barbados was the only place outside the present United States ever visited by the first President of that country.

George Washington's House, Barbados.

133
A rather later card showing 'George Washington's House, Barbados' -- obviously an entirely different building! This appears to be the building at the corner of Bay Street and Chelsea Road, which was long claimed as Washington's house, but which was not built until many years after his visit.

HISTORIC BUILDINGS AND MONUMENTS

134
A wonderful fake: the 'Tomb of Paleologus, St. John's Churchyard, Barbados'. Ferdinando Paleologus (who died in 1670, not 1678 as is stated on the tombstone) is buried here, and his alleged descent 'from ye imperial lyne of ye last Christian Emperors of Greece' may actually be authentic, but the mock seventeenth-century tombstone we see here, with its inscription adapted from that on the tomb of Paleologus's father in England, was erected in 1906. This postcard was probably published soon afterwards. Tourists were presumably just as impressed in the early years of this century as they are now!

135
The Fern Houses in Queen's Park, Barbados, were probably erected at about the time the area became a public park in 1909. These delicate, ephemeral structures have long gone, while Queen's Park House, built in the late 18th century and the official residence of the officer commanding the British garrison in Barbados until the British troops were withdrawn in 1905, which is visible at the left, still stands. It now houses an art gallery and a small theatre.

136
Norham, in Tweedside: an elaborate Barbadian suburban mansion, now demolished. The postcard dates from about 1905.

137
The Colonial Bank in Broad Street, Bridgetown -- long since replaced by a rather similar building belonging to the bank's successor, Barclays.

HISTORIC BUILDINGS AND MONUMENTS

138
The Police Courts in Bridgetown are still used as law courts and look more or less as they do in this card, though a little more dilapidated; scarcely any trace remains of the coats of arms visible here on the pediments.

Police Courts, Barbados.

St. Michael's Almshouse.

139
The St. Michael's Almshouse, Barbados. Now the geriatric hospital.

140
Even the Leper Asylum in Barbados seems to have been thought a good subject for a postcard. The buildings now house the island's Department of Archives.

141
The Citadel at Brimstone Hill, St. Kitts -- a view which has probably not changed a great deal from the eighteenth century to the present.

HISTORIC BUILDINGS AND MONUMENTS

142
Government House, St. Lucia.

143
Nicholas Abbey, Barbados. A fine seventeenth-century mansion in the northern parish of St. Peter, which is happily still with us -- almost identical views appear on postcards sold today. Note the rather crude retouching on the windows.

GLIMPSES OF OUR PAST

POST CARD

The Address only here

7

CITYSCAPES AND STREET SCENES

GLIMPSES OF OUR PAST

144
Bird's eye view of Bridgetown by Alfred Bayley. Broad Street runs diagonally from just above the bottom left of the picture; the old Barbados Mutual building and the tower of St. Mary's Church are clearly visible in the background.

145
Views of ports from the sea would appear to have been popular. This card shows Basseterre, St. Kitts. The Treasury Building (at the right of the picture) dates from the 1890's and is still a prominent landmark.

CITYSCAPES AND STREET SCENES

146
The waterfront at Roseau, Dominica. Card published locally by J.R.H. Bridgewater, Druggist but this specimen postally used from St. Kitts to Barbados in 1910.

147
Stabroek Market and the Stellings, Georgetown, British Guiana. One of many Caribbean cards from photographs taken by Algernon Aspinall, and published by him in England. He was the author of an early tourist handbook called the *Pocket Guide to the West Indies* which was first published in 1907 and continued to be issued in revised editions for many years.

148
Basse-Terre, Guadeloupe.

149
Nice view in St. Thomas, D.W.I. or, in other words, what was still the Danish West Indies until 1917. The Danish *Brevkort* for Postcard is printed on the reverse, and the Danish flag is visible on the staff in the middle foreground. But somehow the Stars and Stripes flying above the building on the left is more prominent -- a sign of things to come.

CITYSCAPES AND STREET SCENES

150
A view of the Queen Emma Bridge in Willemstad, Curaçao, postally used in 1903. There is now a more modern bridge, but it still swings open to admit sea-going vessels into the St. Anna Bay, and the Punda waterfront has not changed much.

151
Otrabanda -- literally the other side of the St. Anna Bay, on an undivided back card of about the same date. *Calle ancha* is of course Breedestraat (or Broad Street); you are not likely to see a man leading a horse here nowadays, but many older buildings survive in Breedestraat and in other parts of the Otrabanda district of Willemstad.

GLIMPSES OF OUR PAST

152
A fine view in Paramaribo, from one of a number of cards apparently bought in Suriname by a visitor in 1903 and posted by him on his return to England. The detail visible on the costumes and the horse-drawn vehicles make this a particularly attractive card.

153
Early undivided back card of the Market Square in St. George's, Grenada. The detail repays study with a magnifying glass.

CITYSCAPES AND STREET SCENES

154
Not so much is happening in this street in Roseau, but it is a nice scene by the Antiguan photographer José Anjo, and the fact that this example has been postally used from Dominica to England in 1904 is a plus.

155
A street in St. John's, Antigua. No indication of the photographer, but published in England as a Raphael Tuck & Sons West Indian view Postcard.

156
Trafalgar Square and Gardens, Barbados -- about 1906. The horse-drawn tram, the mule-cart and the hand-barrow laden with what look like bags of sugar, the schooners and lighters in the Careenage, and the exceptionally crisp detail, all make this card a fascinating glimpse into a world which has utterly vanished. Published by the local firm of J. R. H. Seifert & Co. Ltd., but printed in Germany.

157
Tudor Street, looking south. Another Bridgetown scene of about the same date, this time by W. G. Cooper. There are still many old buildings in Bridgetown, but most have been drastically altered since this date, and the overhanging galleries which were once so characteristic are now scarce.

158
The electric tram is the most prominent feature of this busy Jamaican market scene, but many other details are worth a closer look.

159
Much of downtown Kingston had to be rebuilt after the 1907 earthquake. This attractive card published by H. S. Duperly & Son perhaps appeared soon after the buildings were completed.

GLIMPSES OF OUR PAST

160
Another view of the same area, in the 'Greetings from Jamaica' series published by A. Duperly & Son. The fact that the card is printed in the USA rather than Germany might suggest a slightly later date, perhaps around 1920, but note how horse-drawn vehicles still predominate.

161
Frederick Street in Port of Spain, on an undivided back card. Too much road surface in the foreground for this to be a great piece of photography, but it shows clearly how things have changed!

162
The High Street in San Fernando, Trinidad. This card was published locally by J. Dalgliesh, whose sign is visible about half-way down the right-hand side of the street.

163
Bridge over the Castries River, St. Lucia.

GLIMPSES OF OUR PAST

164
Locally published card of the Rue Lallouette in Cayenne, French Guiana. Not postally used, but originally bought by someone who took the trouble to rubber-stamp the date '26 Jul 1929' on the back.

165
Beautiful panorama of Port of Spain, on an 'undivided back' card postally used from Trinidad to England in 1907.

POST CARD

The Address only here

HOUSING

166
Early 'undivided back' card, captioned *Type of Residence, Barbados*. The hand-written message reads in part 'Love & good wishes for 1907'. Note what appears to be the lady of the house giving her instructions to the gardener; the figure of another gardener is partly visible at the right-hand edge of the card.

167
A Country Residence, Barbados. A plantation house in the grand style, with family members posing on the open verandah and in upstairs windows. The card has a divided back, and so is probably published a little later than the previous one, about 1910.

168
A City Residence, Bridgetown, Barbados. Same local publisher (W. L. Johnson & Co. Ltd.) as the previous card, and probably published at the same time. The house appears to be one which is still standing on the outskirts of Belleville, just below Government House; it has changed little in the past eighty years.

169
Group of Peasants showing type of residence, Barbados. The use of the word 'Peasants' in the caption is questionable, since most Barbadians of the period were landless agricultural labourers, who rented the spots on which their houses stood. The picture shows a classic Bajan chattel house, so constructed that it could be easily taken apart into sections and moved to a new location. Note the fact that the building is made of unpainted boards, the four-hipped roof of wooden shingles, and the solid door and window shutters. A few almost identical houses are still to be found in rural Barbados.

170
Another Barbadian card, showing *Agricultural Labors & Dwellings (sic)*. The roof is gable-ended, rather than four-hipped, and the shutters have jalousies instead of being solid, but the house is the same basic type as that shown in the previous card. At most, it would have had two rooms, but it is quite possible that it was home to all ten of those shown in the picture. This card was also published in a coloured version.

171
Still from Barbados, this *Labourer's Cottage* of about the same date is much more crudely constructed. By this period, thatched roofs seem to have been rare in Barbados in comparison to shingled ones. Somebody's aunt sent them this particular card 'with love & best wishes for a jolly Christmas'.

172
A slightly later card (possibly 1920s) showing a *Native Thatched Hut -- Nassau, Bahamas.* Like the Barbadian examples, this is neatly built, using lumber probably imported from North America.

173
Fine undivided back card, postally used from Trinidad to England in 1904, showing *A Native Home, Trinidad.* Note the board construction, and the jalousied windows at the front, which might perhaps have glass panes in their middle sections, though this is not certain from the picture. The roof is thatched, but a close look suggests that part of the side of the house has been shingled -- a standard means of providing additional weather proofing.

174
A card from the Jamaican firm of A. Duperly & Sons, showing a *Negro Hut*. Undivided back, postally used from Jamaica to England in 1906. What appears to be a section made of boards is visible between the two figures to the right, but the basic construction of the house is almost certainly what Jamaicans call 'Spanish Wall', that is, wattle and daub.

175
A slightly later card, from Duperly's 'Greetings from Jamaica' series. Some of the plastering on the buildings has come off, showing the wattle construction clearly. The caption is *'Resting after a day's work on banana field'*.

HOUSING

176
Native Hut, St. Lucia. Not a scrap of imported timber here. All the materials for this carefully constructed but extremely basic dwelling would have been gathered within walking distance of the site.

177
East Indian huts at Houston, East Bank, Demerara, Guyana.

178
A thatched hut in Curaçao and its inhabitants. Perhaps about 1920.

179
A real photo card of *A Village Street* in Jamaica. The back has 'Canadian Pacific Cruise' printed on it, and the scrawled message 'We arrive here tomorrow It was very hot in Panama' suggests it was bought on board ship, though there is a Kingston postmark dated 1932.

180
A village scene in St. Kitts, published by A. Moure Losada, Basseterre. I have seen another specimen of this card postally used in 1933, but the general appearance of the card, and the 'Printed in Saxony' on the back suggest it was produced earlier, before the First World War. The design of the address side is almost identical with that of the card showing the Basseterre sugar factory (52), and the same typefaces are used.

181
Country road in Grenada at the beginning of the century. This type of scene is much rarer on postcards than urban street scenes. There is a nice pan-Caribbean feel to this card -- it was produced by the Antiguan photographer José Anjo, and this specimen was postally used from St. Kitts to the USA in 1909. The usual admonition 'The address only to be written on this side' appears on the undivided back, and so a whole budget of family news has been crammed onto the available space on the picture side.

POST CARD

The Address only here

9
DISASTERS

182
After the hurricane of 1899, Montserrat. One of Algernon Aspinall's 'West Indian Picture Postcards', published in England.

183
Trinidadian card, showing the *Red House* (the main government offices) on fire, 23 March 1903, following the famous 'Water Riots' when an increase in water rates sparked off popular protest.

DISASTERS

184
Exceptional view of Port Royal Street, Kingston, after the earthquake of 1907. This card was printed and published in Britain.

185
Ruins of Bay St. Stancheon. A comparatively minor disaster -- a fire in Bridgetown, Barbados.

111

GLIMPSES OF OUR PAST

186 & 187
Perhaps the ultimate disaster cards for the Caribbean collector are those issued in the aftermath of the volcanic explosion of Mont Pelé in Martinique on 8 May 1902. One of the most horrific natural disasters in history, the explosion completely destroyed the town of St. Pierre, the island's main port, in a matter of minutes, killing nearly 30,000 people. Only two of those in the town survived. The disaster created a market for pictures of the town as it was, such as these cards from a booklet of twelve issued by a local publisher under the title 'St. Pierre avant la catastrophe.' One of them clearly shows the enormous cloud of volcanic dust which hung over Mont Pelé for two weeks before the explosion, giving ample warning of what was to come. However, the local authorities assured the inhabitants that there was nothing to worry about, and encouraged them to remain in the town — because they wanted voters to be around for an election.

St. Pierre was eventually rebuilt after the disaster, but has never regained its former importance.

112

POST CARD

The Address only here

10

RELIGION, FESTIVALS AND ENTERTAINMENT

188
Churches were a popular subject for postcards, ranging from grander specimens like the Anglican Cathedral in St. John's, Antigua ...

189
... to the more humble, like Fig-Tree Church in Nevis. This Church is famous for housing the original register recording the marriage of the British naval hero, Horatio Nelson, to a local beauty, the widowed Mrs. Nisbet, in 1787 ...

RELIGION, FESTIVALS AND ENTERTAINMENT

190
... or the chapel at the Roman Catholic abbey of Mount St. Benedict in Trinidad, seen here on a card published in Belgium and postally used from Trinidad to Holland in 1933.

191
Good view of the Anglican church in Roseau, Dominica, since destroyed by Hurricane David. On the back of the card is printed the legend 'Sold by Hotel de Paz, Dominica'.

192
Usually postcards just show the buildings, but this fine view of St. Lucy's Church, Barbados, (probably 1907, but this specimen postally used in 1917) shows people going to church. Note the children on foot, and the horse and buggy with its top-hatted coachman.

St. Lucy's Church, Barbados
J. R. H. Seifert & Co., Ltd., Barbados.

Waraputa Mission - Essequebo with the Bishop of British Guiana.

6760 printed in Germany H. K. L. v. Ziegesar, Georgetown.

193
Undivided back card showing *Waraputa Mission -- Essequebo [sic] with the Bishop of British Guiana*. A number of religious groups worked for the conversion of Guyana's Amerindians. The figure on the right in the light-coloured suit is possibly Bishop Swaby, who was the Anglican Bishop of British Guiana before becoming Bishop of Barbados.

RELIGION, FESTIVALS AND ENTERTAINMENT

194
Card of about 1907 (postally used in 1915) showing the Anglican Archbishop of the West Indies, Enos Nuttal, (on the right) and Bishop Swaby of Barbados in the grounds of Bishop's Court, Barbados.

195
View of the Empire Theatre in Trinidad. A view of the interior with a show going on would have been even nicer, but I have yet to come across such a card from the Caribbean.

Trafalgar Day, Barbados, 1905. Nelson's Statue.

196
Grand celebrations were held in Barbados for the centenary of the Battle of Trafalgar in 1905, and Bridgetown's statue of Lord Nelson was decorated for the occasion. Note the wreath suspended over the statue's head, and the lettering round the arch, giving Nelson's last words: 'Thank God I have done my duty'. The serial number on the reverse of the card suggests that it was not manufactured (in Germany) until 1907, and this specimen was postally used in Barbados in 1912.

197
The Belleville Tennis Club in Barbados, from a card probably from before the First World War. Rather obviously an 'exclusive' institution!

BELLEVILLE TENNIS CLUB. BARBADOS, B.W.I.

RELIGION, FESTIVALS AND ENTERTAINMENT

198
Fine offical photograph of the West Indies cricket team, 1933. This was the team which made the second official tour of Englind after the West Indies had been accorded Test status in 1928. (The first tour of England by a West Indian side had been in 1900.) Three Tests were played, of which England won two, with the other being drawn — the first draw the West Indies achieved in England. Learie Constantine, who contributed significantly to the result of the drawn second Test at Old Trafford, is not included in the picture. Other significant performances on the West Indies side were those of the young Barbadian fast bowler, E. A. Martindale, and the illustrious Jamaican batsman, George Headley.

199
Fine card with undivided back from Trinidad, showing the Queen's Park Cricket Ground and Pavilion. A match in progress, but -- alas! -- no indication of who is playing. The Queen's Park Savannah saw many famous games, including (in September 1893) the first inter-colonial cricket match between Trinidad and Barbados. Barbados won.

200
The Rockley Golf and Country Club, Barbados. Probably somewhat later than the previous card.

201
Sailing Boats, Fontabelle B'dos, postally used from Barbados to the USA in 1909. This bit of coastline has changed completely with the building of the deep water harbour. However, the interest of this card (not unfortunately as clear as one would like) is the fact that two, and possibly three, of the figures appear to be holding model sailing boats. These boats, home-made and hand-carved and rigged, were once a popular pastime, but are now seldom seen.

RELIGION, FESTIVALS AND ENTERTAINMENT

203
Rather less of an establishment figure is this *'Negro playing his guitar'* on a Barbadian card used about 1912 (postmark unclear). Although posed in a studio, he seems to be one of the strolling minstrels who were once familiar street characters, but who are now almost extinct in their original form.

202
Bandsman of West Indian Regiment, Barbados. Note the Zouave uniform, which is still worn by the band of the Barbados Regiment.

204
Carnival Steel Band, Trinidad, B.W.I., apparently showing the early stages of the development of the pan -- the original form of the oil-drums is clearly visible. The Union Jack may possibly suggest a date during the Second World War.

205
Sanitized for tourist consumption. A steel band waits to greet ship's passengers at the Pier Head in Bridgetown, Barbados. Perhaps about 1950.

RELIGION, FESTIVALS AND ENTERTAINMENT

206
Nightclub entertainment in the glory days of Cuba's tourist industry. Nice real photo card from 1940s or 1950s showing 'Cuban typical rumba'.

GLIMPSES OF OUR PAST

POST CARD

The Address only here

11

KEEPING CONTROL

GLIMPSES OF OUR PAST

207
This card of about 1907 was published by a jeweller in Georgetown and shows a panoramic view of the penal settlement on the Mazaruni River in Guyana.

208
A detachment of the Barbados Volunteers, a body of part-time troops formed in 1902 as the withdrawal of the last of the British garrison stationed in the island became imminent. Along with the police, they played an important role in the suppression of the popular disturbances generally referred to as the 1937 Riots. The Volunteers later developed into the Barbados Regiment (1948), which continues to exist as the reserve unit of the Barbados Defence Force (formally established 1978). This card probably about 1910.

209
If the resources available to the local authorities were not enough, they knew that they could always call on the colonial power. This card by the Antiguan photographer José Anjo shows H.M.S. Patrol Fleet at Anchor off Rat Island during Riot, March 1918.

210
Another view of the Royal Navy in the Caribbean, this time anchored off Basseterre, St. Kitts. Difficult to date this card with any precision, but the Royal Navy was called in to assist in suppressing unrest on several occasions in the first half of the century, particularly during the series of protests which swept through the Caribbean in the later 1930s.

211
Real photo card showing, according to the caption, USS North Dakota in Barbados, Feb 15 1920. There are in fact several ships visible, and somebody has pencilled on the back of the card 'U.S.S. Fla., British cruiser, and U.S.S. N.D. at Bridgetown, Barbadoes' (sic).

212
The colonial infantry barracks in Cayenne, French Guiana, from a 1920s card.

POST CARD

The Address only here

12
PORTRAITS

213
For the original publisher this card (perhaps 1920s or 1930s) shows *Cabbage Palms, Barbados, B.W.I.* It is perhaps not too fanciful to suggest that the old woman and the boy, like the man farther away, were seen (if at all) only as intrusions into the landscape, though they are what is probably most likely to catch the attention of the modern viewer.

Cabbage Palms, Barbados, B. W. I.

214
Group of *Plantation Labourers, Barbados* on a locally published card. The photographer has paid no attention to the effect of the lighting on the faces of his subjects; it is impossible to make out anything of the features of most of those in the picture.

215
On the other hand, distance rather than bad lighting has the same effect on this card from the same Barbadian publisher as the preceding one; these Harrison College cadets may have been children of privilege, but they have been reduced to the same faceless anonymity.

216
Group of Amerindians in the Ireng Valley, British Guiana. Card postally used to Holland in 1905.

217
Another group of Amerindians, this time from Suriname; about 1903.

218
Card of about the same date, showing group of East Indians from Suriname.

PORTRAITS

219
Artist's impression of *Coolie Girl*, Demerara. Card postally used from Guyana to Barbados in 1919, but the generous space for a message on the view side and the fact that it was originally an undivided back, suggest that it may have been produced ten or twelve years earlier.

220
Another card from the same source as Nos. 217 and 218, bought in Suriname in 1903 by a visitor and posted in England on his return. This shows a group of the Maroons, descendants of escaped African slaves from the interior of Suriname; the sender has translated the Dutch caption 'Boschneger' as 'Bushniggers' and added the would-be facetious comment 'My fellow Citizens'.

221
Magnificent studio portrait of Creole woman from Suriname in traditional dress; postally used to Holland in 1906.

222
Another attractive costume shot, this time of *A St. Lucia Belle*. An undivided back card, not much later than about 1905.

223
The woman with two little pigs comes from Barbados, about 1910. The background looks heavily retouched and the original caption has 'Pic Selles' for 'Pig Seller'.

224
A card of similar date from Trinidad. The woman looks slightly apprehensive; note the way the original caption emphasizes her anonymity as a *'West Indian Type'*.

GLIMPSES OF OUR PAST

225
'Greetings from Jamaica' card showing group of women *Going to Market with Yams and Canes, Constant Spring Road*.

226
The Native Choir from Jamaica. Card published in England, and postally used there in 1906; the message on the back mentions 'We heard this Jamaica Choir sing at the Castle the other night'.

227
Real photo card of a colonial governor and party; where is another question -- the dealer from whom I bought this and the next card thought it might be British Honduras. The length of the women's skirts suggests a date in the 1930s.

228
Some of the same people -- at the beach!

GLIMPSES OF OUR PAST

229
A Tuck's 'West Indian view Postcard' of a group of children, captioned *The rising Generation, West Indies.* Published in England and postally used there in 1904.

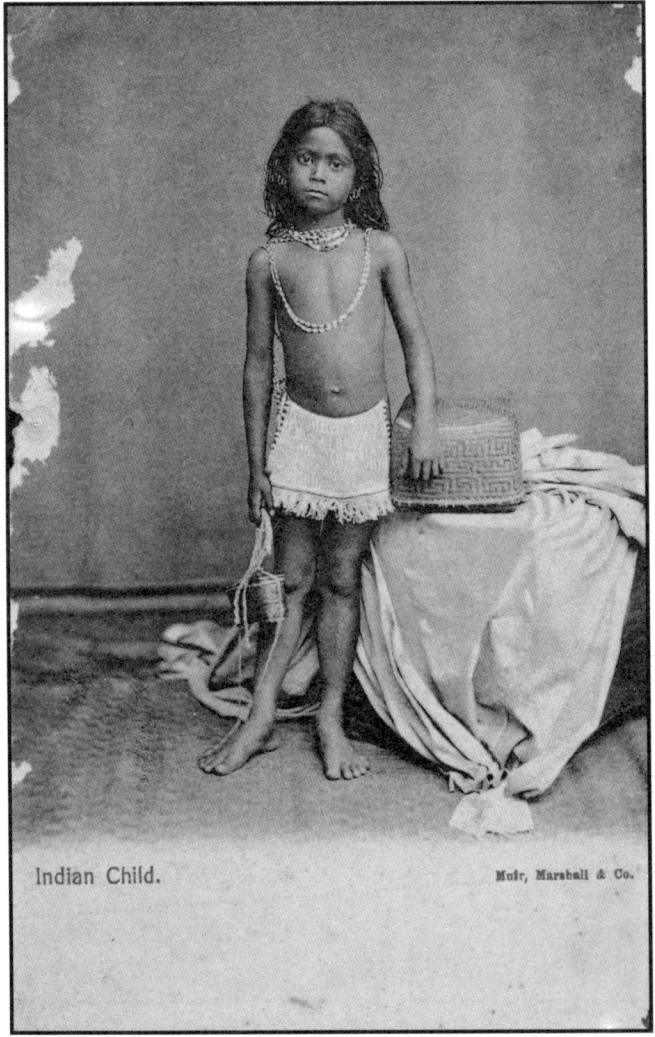

230
Indian Child posed in a photographer's studio in Trinidad.

PORTRAITS

231
Card with embossed floral pattern and two real photo vignettes of the same pair of children, captioned *Loyal subjects of the King*. Printed in England, but published in Jamaica.

232
This Fisherboy with Conger Eel from Barbados was probably photographed in the 1920s.

233
Group of children on a card published in Barbados in the 1920s or 1930s with the caption *Natives on Railway Line*.

234
Card from St. Thomas, Danish West Indies (printed in Austria), showing *Group of Natives*. Postally used from St. Thomas to France in 1908.

235
These children are a *Native Group* on a Barbadian card postally used to Canada in 1924.

236
Undivided back card from Grenada. There is nothing inherently implausible about either the old man or his shack, but the original caption, *Uncle Tom's Cabin, Grenada, W.I.*, suggests a cheap appeal to spurious sentimentality.

237
This looks posed by a photographer seeking an 'exotic' shot -- does anybody really suck cane like this? The original caption -- *'Native sucking cane, Barbados'* -- adds to this impression.

238
Train line barber, Barbados. A nice shot -- but was it deliberately set up by the photographer?

239
By contrast, this hair-cutting scene on a Sunday Morning, Demerara, looks a lot more authentic, even though the standing man and the children are having a good stare at the photographer. Note the barracks-type housing.

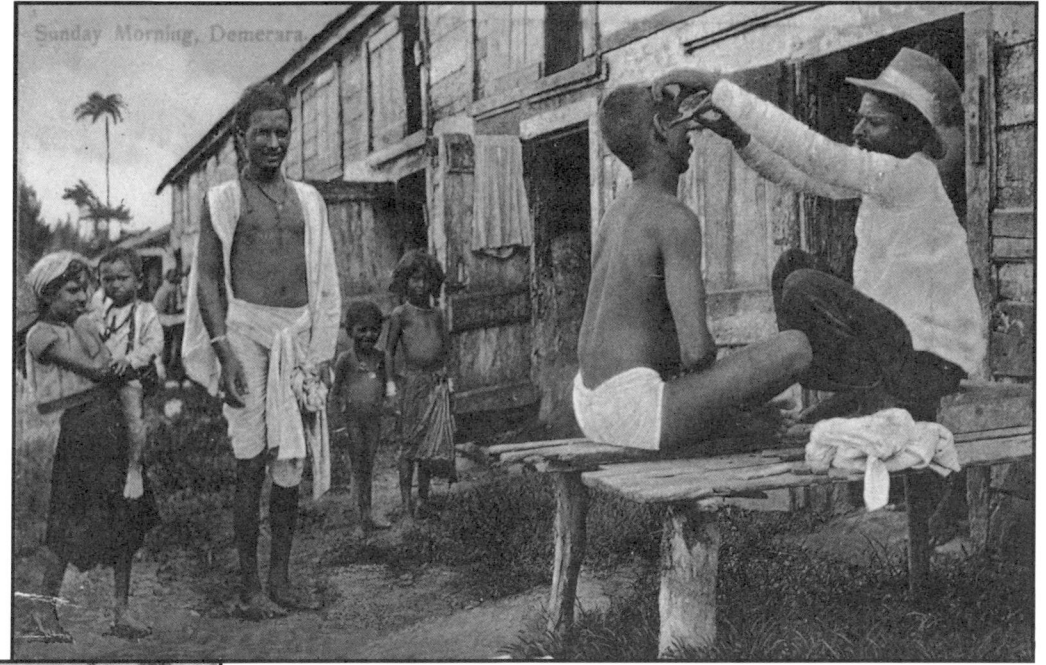

240
Group of Boys is the original caption; no indication of photographer, printer or publisher, but the card was postally used in Barbados in 1907. I have seen what seems to be a slightly later version of this card, with the publisher given as G. A. Plimmer, Barbados, and the caption 'BARBADOS. WHARF RATS.' The more you look at the children's faces, the more enigmatic and disturbing they become. Somebody got this group together and got them to stay still long enough for the picture to be taken -- what were they thinking? What was the photographer thinking? But the most extraordinary detail is the contrast between the image and the message written on the back: 'Wishing you a bright & happy Xmas & New Year ...'

If the bug bites...

The illustrations in this book show only a very small sample of the many thousands of postcards with Caribbean subjects produced in the first half of the twentieth century.

If they have aroused your interest and you would like to see more, you may find that museums, national trusts, and educational institutions in your country have at least some old postcards which they have acquired over the years. You should bear in mind that such organizations are usually unable to put everything on display to the public, and that you may have to make an appointment to see special collections such as postcards.

If you decide to start collecting postcards yourself, you will be embarking on a fascinating and comparatively inexpensive hobby. Many collectors start out by taking anything and everything, but sooner or later most end up specializing. You can decide to collect cards from only in Caribbean country, or cards showing the sugar industry, or cricket, or almost any subject that is of particular interest to you. When you begin to meet other collectors, all those miscellaneous cards you acquired earlier will come in useful for exchanging.

It is worth telling all your friends and relations of your new enthusiasm - you never know what treasures somebody's aunt might be willing to let you have. For the most part, however, you will have to buy your cards. The local antique shop is a good bet, and cards will occasionally turn up in auctions of household effects. Inevitably, cards with local subjects cost more. You can expect to pay more from Trinidadian cards in Trinidad, Barbadian ones in Barbados and so on.

If you travel to Europe or North America, you will be able specialist dealers who will often have a very large stock for you to choose from, and in many cases you will have a good chance of finding worthwhile Caribbean cards at prices less than you would have to pay in the caribbean. Some of these dealers will be happy to do business with you by post if you give them a good idea of what you want. If you are looking for cards from St. Kitts, you are wasting everybody's time if you ask for "old Caribbean cards." You will be offered a lot of material you don't want to buy and the dealer will soon lose interest in you.

For where to find dealers, information on postcard fairs, as well as articles on postcards and postcard collecting, an invaluable source is the magazine *Picture Postcard Monthly*, obtainable Reflections of a Bygone Age, 15 Debdale Lane, Keyworth, Nottingham NG12 5HT, England. For the North American market, see the magazine *Today's Collector*, Krause Publications Inc., 700 East State Street, Iola, WI 54990, U.S.A.

Prices for postcards are very much a matter of supply and demand. Cards from some islands are significantly harder to find than others, and prices reflect this. In general, expect to pay more for interesting cards than dull ones. A busy street scene with lots of people and good detail will cost more than a view of the same street photographed empty. However, you should remember that what appears to be dull to one collector may fascinate. Certain subjects, such as railways and windmills, appeal to some collectors no matter what countries they come from. On a used card, a rare stamp or unusual postmark may add significantly to the price.

One of the most important factors in determining the price is the condition. For this reason, you should protect the value of your investment by storing your collection properly. Many different types of postcards albums are available, and any reputable dealer or experienced collector will be happy to advise you. Most importantly, you should be aware that cards can be permanently damaged if they are stored in certain types of plastics. Make sure you ask for accessories that are PVC-free.

Many cards seventy or eighty years old can be obtained looking as good as new. Worn or damaged cards accordingly command much lower prices, and there are plenty of collectors who simply refuse to buy cards in less than perfect condition. My own view is that, if the card is sufficiently interesting you should buy it anyway, even if it has a couple of wormholes or a torn corner. A better specimen may eventually turn up, or it may not. I remember seeing in the collection of a National Trust in the Caribbean a card which had been torn right across so that half of it was missing. It was preserved with as much care as the rest, for it was the only specimen of that particular card they had, and the Trust's Director felt that half a card was better than no card at all!

Happy hunting!

INDEX OF PLACES

(Numbers refer to those of postcards illustrated)

Antigua
13, 155, 188, 209

Bahamas
76, 115, 172

Barbados
1a, 1b, 3, 5, 6, 8a, 8b, 9, 10, 14, 15, 17, 18, 21, 24a, 24b, 27, 30-32, 34, 37, 38, 40, 42a, 42b, 43, 50, 51, 53, 54, 55a, 55b, 61, 63, 72, 73, 77, 80, 81, 87, 88, 90, 91, 93-96, 101, 106-110, 116, 124, 126, 127, 131-140, 143, 144, 156, 157, 166-171, 185, 192, 194, 196, 197, 200, -203, 205, 208, 211, 213-215, 223, 232, 233, 235, 237, 238, 240

Belgium
2

Belize
227, 228

Bermuda
20, 71, 114

British Guiana
- see Guyana

British Honduras
- see Belize

Carriacou
39

cayenne
- see French Guiana

Cuba
104, 117, 129, 206

Curaçao
64, 85, 150, 151, 178

Danish West Indies
- see under St. Croix and St. Thomas

Dominica
146, 154, 191

Dominican Republic
16, 36, 128

Federation of the West Indies
19

French Guiana
164, 212

Grenada
12a, 12b, 47, 49, 56, 57, 59, 89, 102, 105, 111, 153, 181, 236

Guadeloupe
75, 148

Guyana
11a, 11b, 79, 98, 130, 147, 177, 193, 207, 216, 219, 239

Haiti
35

Jamaica
7, 28, 29, 41a, 41b, 44, 45, 46a, 46b, 67, 68, 69, 70, 82, 118-122, 158-160, 174, 175, 179, 184, 225, 226, 231

Martinique
74, 186, 187

Montserrat
62, 182

Netherlands Antilles
- see Curaçao

Nevis
189

Puerto Rico
25

St. Croix(USVI)
60

St. Kitts
52, 141, 145, 180, 210

St. Lucia
23a, 23b, 48, 66, 86, 142, 163, 176, 222

St. Thomas(USVI)
149, 234

St. Vincent
112

Suriname
78, 97, 152, 217, 218, 220, 221

Trinidad
4, 22a, 22b, 26, 58, 65, 83, 84, 92, 99, 100, 113, 123, 161, 162, 165, 173, 183, 190, 195, 199, 204, 224, 230

Unidentified
33

United States Vergin Islands
- see under St. Croix and St. Thomas

West Indies (General)
103, 125, 198, 229,
- see also Federation of the West Indies